BABIES & TODDLERS
Good food

THE AUSTRALIAN
Women's Weekly

babies and toddlers

contents

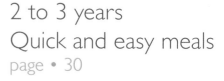

good food

learning about food for infants

Let's be honest – food and eating are not only a vitally important part of living, they're also one of life's great pleasures. Having spent your whole life eating, and developing your own tastes and nutritional standards, it's now time to begin to pass your accrued wisdom onto the latest addition to your family. And while this might seem like a solemn task (and in the days to come, possibly a rather thankless one at times), there is no doubt that with a little commonsense and a large dose of humour, you will find it not only manageable but also very rewarding as you watch your baby learn about food and the wonderfully sociable process of eating.

When you're poring over pyramid charts of the five food groups and agonising over baby's lack of interest in your latest culinary offering, it's very easy to lose sight of the fact that learning about food can, and should, be fun.

The important thing is to use this book as a reference, and not as a set of rules that must be slavishly obeyed. Babies are individuals. They do things at different rates and early on can display very definite likes and dislikes. For every baby that eats cottage cheese with undisguised relish, there will be another (yours) who spits it in your eye every time. You can take it personally, or you can serve something else.

The trick is to remain flexible, be guided by your baby and, above all, try not to worry too much. Learning about food is an extended process and the least sensible approach is to feel guilty because *your* little bundle of joy appears to have been born with a cynical disregard for the five food groups. Go with the flow – your reward, in the short term, will be a baby who is soon eating family meals with you happily and, in the long term, the establishment of good eating habits for a lifetime.

Mums need feeding too!

In all the excitement of starting life with a new baby, it's often easy for new mothers to forget that they need a bit of special looking after too! Your body has just completed a nine-month marathon, your hormones have run away to join the circus, every single thing a new baby does can be completely terrifying if you're seeing it for the first time and, more than anything else, you're tired, tired, tired!

Babies can be hard work and it's vital to keep up your own reserves of energy to stay equal to the task. This is especially important if you are breastfeeding, but *all* new mothers need to make sure their diet is adequate.

In those sleep-deprived early days, it can be tempting to skip meals altogether in order to snatch 40 winks, but this is unwise as it will only lead you further and further into a spiral of fatigue.

If you're too tired to cook, try at least to whiz up a high-energy drink and sip a glass or two while you're resting or feeding the baby. Better still, if your partner, friends or family ask what they can do to help, tell them a meal you can reheat or store in the freezer would be manna from heaven!

OAT BRAN, BANANA AND PECAN MUFFINS

oat bran, banana and pecan muffins

You will need about 2 large (460g) overripe bananas for this recipe.

3/4 cup (120g) wholemeal self-raising flour
I cup (150g) white self-raising flour
1/2 teaspoon mixed spice
1/2 cup (60g) oat bran
2 tablespoons brown sugar
1/2 cup (60g) pecans, chopped coarsely
I cup mashed banana
1/4 cup (60ml) vegetable oil
2 eggs, beaten lightly
1/3 cup (80ml) skim milk
2 tablespoons golden syrup
12 pecans, extra

Grease 12-hole (1/3-cup/80ml-capacity) muffin pan.

Sift flours and spice into large bowl; stir in bran, sugar and chopped pecans. Add banana then combined oil, eggs, milk and syrup; stir just until combined. Divide mixture among pan holes; top with extra pecans. Bake in moderately hot oven 20 minutes; turn onto wire rack to cool.

MAKES 12

Best made on day of serving

tuna and ricotta potatoes

2 large (600g) potatoes
95g can tuna in oil, drained, flaked
1/2 cup (100g) ricotta cheese
2 green onions, chopped finely
2 teaspoons baby capers
I teaspoon finely grated lemon rind
2 tablespoons finely chopped parsley
I clove garlic, crushed

Scrub potatoes well; pierce skin all over. Bake potatoes in moderate oven about 1 1/2 hours or until tender. When cool enough to handle, cut 1cm off top of each potato; scoop out and reserve flesh, leaving 5mm shell. Combine potato flesh with remaining ingredients in medium bowl; divide mixture between potato shells. Place potatoes on oven tray; bake, uncovered, about 15 minutes or until hot. Serve topped with yogurt, if desired.

MAKES 2

Best made just before serving

TUNA AND RICOTTA POTATOES

fruit cup crush

I large (600g) mango, chopped coarsely
I cup (185g) coarsely chopped watermelon
1/4 medium (300g) pineapple, chopped coarsely
I tablespoon sugar
I cup (250ml) orange juice

Blend or process fruit and sugar until smooth; add juice, blend until combined.

MAKES 4 CUPS (1 litre)

Best made just before serving

banana smoothie

I medium (200g) banana, chopped coarsely
3/4 cup (180ml) milk
I tablespoon yogurt
2 tablespoons honey
I scoop (40g) vanilla ice-cream
4 ice cubes

Blend or process all ingredients until smooth.

MAKES 2 CUPS (500ml)

Best made just before serving

mixed berry shake

I cup (150g) strawberries
1/2 cup (70g) raspberries
1/2 cup (75g) blueberries
I tablespoon honey-flavoured yogurt
2 teaspoons sugar
3/4 cup (180ml) milk
I scoop (40g) vanilla ice-cream

Blend or process all berries until pureed; strain through fine sieve into jug. Blend or process berry puree with remaining ingredients until smooth.

MAKES 2 CUPS (500ml)

Best made just before serving

MIXED BERRY SHAKE

BANANA SMOOTHIE

FRUIT CUP CRUSH

0 to 4 months
OFF TO A GOOD START

Mother's milk

Breastmilk is what nature designed for new babies. It contains exactly what they need in terms of nutrients, comes in perfect germ-free containers, and is always on hand at precisely the right temperature. Given these impeccable advantages, it would have to be the natural choice for a baby's first nutrition, wherever possible.

However, sometimes breastfeeding is just not an option, and if you are bottle-feeding your baby, you should take comfort from the knowledge that today's infant formulas are the nearest thing that science can get to breastmilk. And of course, whether you choose breast or bottle, almost as important as nutrition in these early weeks is the wonderful intimacy that develops between you and your baby as feeding patterns are established. Everyone tells you about feeding, burping, colic and nappy rash. Nobody has ever come close to describing adequately that exquisite moment of communication when your gaze is held firmly by this extraordinary little stranger before the eyelids begin to droop with utter satisfaction.

But occasionally, it can be a bit bewildering as well – some babies feed at regular intervals, others seem to want to graze non-stop around the clock, much to the alarm of their poor, sleep-starved mums! Whether you are breastfeeding or bottle-feeding, your local midwife or early childhood community nurse is an invaluable source of help and information for these early days. You'll also meet other new mothers whose own experiences are reassuringly similar to yours.

Thinking about weaning

Milk – your own, or an infant formula – is all the food a baby requires for the first four to six months of life. Deciding when to begin weaning baby onto solid food will depend on your own particular circumstances and should always be a gradual process to give you both time to adjust to the change.

After the simplicity of feeding your baby only milk for as long as six months, the idea of introducing solid food can seem a little daunting, especially as everyone you talk to is suddenly an expert on what to do and how to do it. A well-meaning relative will tell you that a big baby like yours needs solids to make him sleep through the night. Your neighbour will swear that cereals stopped her baby's reflux vomiting, and a woman at the checkout will point out your baby's chewed fists as evidence of excessive hunger. Don't get confused – none of these situations calls for weaning. Be guided by your baby and professional advice, and proceed at your own pace. After all, most people seem to have managed to learn to eat, even those whose mothers had begun to think it might never happen!

First things first

So suddenly we're talking about food instead of just milk – a whole new ball game! There's no need to take a second mortgage for special new equipment, however, whatever glossy catalogues might suggest to the contrary; baby's needs are really still very simple. To start, you'll need small spoons without sharp edges – plastic are ideal – an unbreakable bowl and a supply of bibs – the one thing you can count on is a mess! Depending on the age of your baby, you'll also need a high chair or something else for baby to sit in which is easy to wipe down.

Older toddlers can have their own little chair and table, unless you prefer them to sit on a booster seat at the main table. In either case, it is important to establish a specific location for eating – don't let your toddler walk and eat; make him sit and recognise a meal time and place.

Cooking equipment

Food processors and hand-held blenders are great assets when preparing food for young babies who tend to like their purees absolutely smooth. However, a potato masher, ricer or food mill will also puree soft foods just as well and are less expensive. You can also push small

amounts of soft food through a sieve to eliminate lumps.

Kitchen hygiene

• Make sure you always have clean hands before starting to prepare any food.
• All feeding equipment and cooking utensils should be scrupulously clean, but, unlike bottles and teats, there is no need to sterilise them.

• Use different clean chopping boards for raw meat and cooked foods, for poultry and vegetables, to avoid the risk of contamination.
• When preparing dry cereal, make only as much as required for each meal and discard any leftovers.
• NEVER save any uneaten portion of food from the feeding bowl – baby's saliva will have contaminated the remaining food. Throw it away.

Freezing

• Freeze single portions of food in ice cube trays or simply by dropping serving-sized spoonfuls onto a clean tray. Cover tightly and freeze. Once they are frozen, work quickly to place individual serves in freezer bags. Seal, label, date and return to the freezer.

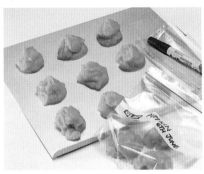

• Do not prepare vast amounts of food – you'll never get through it. Ensure that food is rotated so oldest food is used first.
• Remove only the exact number of cubes required for each meal.
• Always thaw frozen portions of food in the refrigerator.
• Never refreeze thawed food.

MAXIMUM FREEZING TIMES FOR FOOD FOR BABIES	
Fish	3 months
Offal	1 month
Meat	3 months
Poultry	3 months
Fruit	3 months
Vegetables	3 months
Soups	3 months
Breads & cakes	3 months

Reheating and microwaving

Your freezer and microwave oven are invaluable when planning and making food for young children.

When reheating food for your baby, remember that babies do not like hot food. If food has been refrigerated or frozen, it should be briefly brought to a boil then cooled to lukewarm before serving. Freshly made food can be reheated over a saucepan of gently simmering water or in a microwave oven.

While the microwave is a great timesaver when cooking and reheating baby food, great care must be taken. Microwaved food continues to cook after being removed from the oven and can therefore be very hot.

Never serve food cooked or reheated in a microwave oven before stirring then testing it first.

Pause to stir food at intervals during microwave reheating to allow for even heat distribution.

Allow microwaved food to rest outside the oven for several minutes before feeding it to your baby.

FOOD INTOLERANCE AND ALLERGIES

Food intolerance occurs when food is not digested properly, such as gluten intolerance (known as coeliac disease) or milk (lactose) intolerance. A very small number of babies can also suffer true allergic reactions to certain foods.

Symptoms of allergy or intolerance can include swelling and itching around the mouth or throat, diarrhoea, stomach pain, vomiting, runny nose, coughing, eczema, hives, hay fever or asthma. But since most children will exhibit at least some of these symptoms during their babyhood whether they are allergic or not, you should seek medical advice if you think your baby has a problem. It is important to establish whether there actually is an allergy as you might be needlessly eliminating a useful food from the baby's diet.

A tendency to allergy can be hereditary so if you or your immediate family have a history of food reactions, such as asthma, hay fever, eczema or a reaction to peanuts, you should proceed more cautiously when introducing solids. However, most small children will grow out of their allergy and often, if there is a reaction, it can be very mild.

Eggs, peanuts, cow's milk, wheat, shellfish, strawberries and artificial colourings are the foods most commonly linked to allergic reactions and intolerance so you should not offer these foods until baby is a certain age: avoid cow's milk (except infant formula) and wheat products for the first 6 months; avoid egg white and strawberries before 9 to 12 months; leave peanut products until baby is 12 months old (or 5 years if a close relative is allergic). When first adding them to the diet, do so one at a time and in small amounts – if you notice a reaction, wait a month before trying the food again or seek medical advice.

4 to 6 months
WHERE TO BEGIN

As a general guide, you should start to think about introducing solid food between four and six months if . . .
- Your breastfeeding baby is no longer putting on as much weight as he should, despite your efforts to increase supply.
- Your bottle-fed baby is not satisfied with the usual amounts of formula and constantly seems hungry and unsettled.
- Your baby is now six months old and is still fully milk fed.

If you are in any doubt about when to introduce solids, consult your doctor or early-childhood nurse.

starting solids

Initially, solid food should be offered *after* the breast or bottle feed, as milk is still the major source of nourishment. Alternatively, offer half the milk feed, then solid food. This will take the edge off baby's hunger, but he will still be interested in what you have to offer and will be more relaxed and settled. Finish with the remainder of the familiar milk feed. Traditionally, the first food to be offered is rice cereal as it is well tolerated, but you can also start with a little pureed fruit or vegies instead, or mashed ripe banana or avocado.

I If starting with rice cereal, mix 1 to 2 teaspoons with 15ml to 30ml expressed breastmilk, prepared formula or cooled, boiled water until it is a thin paste consistency. Using a spoon without sharp edges (the bowl and spoon do not need to be sterilised), offer baby 1 to 2 teaspoons of the cereal mix at the feed of the day that suits you. Hold the spoon to her lips and allow her to suck the cereal off. Don't push the spoon back into her mouth, it will cause her to gag. Take your time — remember that up until now, your baby has sucked her food, so having a spoon in her mouth is a very new sensation. Repeat this process once a day for a few days.

2 If this step was a success, you can now offer cereal twice a day, for several days, gradually increasing the amount and thickening the consistency to suit your baby, until he is eating up to 1 to 2 tablespoons at a time.

If he consistently refuses the cereal (it *is* a bit like wallpaper paste, after all), then try something else. If he refuses this as well, give up for a week or so, continue with milk only, then try again. Stay calm – and remind yourself there are very few fully milk-fed adults!

3 Next, add a small amount of pureed, stewed apple, pear or very ripe mashed banana to rice cereal. Gradually increase the puree over several days until you are serving equal amounts of cereal and fruit. If this is well tolerated, you can vary one meal by introducing pureed vegetables, usually potato, pumpkin and carrot to start. Offer 1 to 2 teaspoons, slowly increasing the amount over several days to 2 to 3 tablespoons.

4 Gradually increase the variety of vegetables and other foods to allow baby to become accustomed to new tastes and textures. Introduce new foods one at a time and allow a few days on each new food to ensure that baby has no adverse reaction to it, before starting the next.

5 If baby is happily eating two "meals", then you can gradually add a third, so that she is eventually eating 2 to 3 tablespoons of food, three times a day.

pureed apple or pear

1 medium (150g) apple or 1 small (180g) pear, peeled, cored, chopped

Boil, steam or microwave apple or pear until tender; drain over small bowl, reserving 1 tablespoon cooking liquid. Blend or process fruit with cooking liquid or boiled water until smooth.

MAKES 1/2 CUP (125ml)

Storage Covered, in refrigerator, up to 2 days
Freeze Suitable, in individual portions

☺TIP Mix a little of this pureed fruit with yogurt.

pureed potato or pumpkin

1/2 cup (200g) peeled and chopped potato or pumpkin

Boil, steam or microwave potato or pumpkin until tender; drain. Blend or process with enough breast milk, formula or cooled boiled water until of desired consistency.

MAKES 1/2 CUP (125ml)

Storage Covered, in refrigerator, up to 2 days
Freeze Suitable, in individual portions

☺TIP Mashed avocado is an excellent choice for one of your baby's first foods; it's also good blended with a little of the pureed pear or apple.

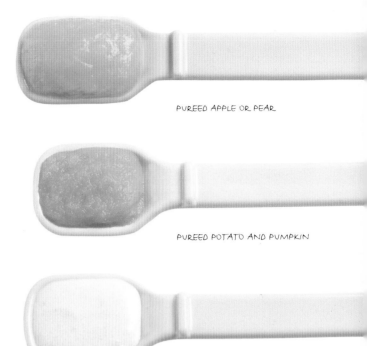

PUREED APPLE OR PEAR

PUREED POTATO AND PUMPKIN

PUREED PEAR WITH YOGURT

Introducing different foods

As your baby grows, so should the number of different foods being offered. If he fusses when given a particular food for the first time, leave it for a while and continue with foods that have already been accepted. But do keep trying new foods at frequent intervals.

You are not, however, running a restaurant for infant gourmands, providing a new taste sensation at every meal! Young babies don't get bored eating the same things repeatedly because they have no prior knowledge about different flavours or textures. This is also true of salt – the taste for salt is acquired. Although you might think the food tastes bland, your baby will not think this and you should not add any salt to food that you prepare for babies under 12 months – excessive sodium has the potential to damage immature kidneys.

Sugar should also be used sparingly – for the sake of your baby's health, you don't want to encourage a "sweet tooth".

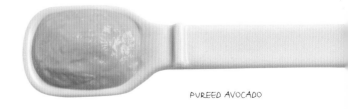

PUREED AVOCADO

BLANCMANGE

photostop It's fun to record baby's first mouthful for posterity. Some babies seem to understand immediately what they're supposed to do, swallow happily and look at you expectantly for more, like a baby bird. Others react as though you've taken an enormous liberty and get a "you must be joking" look that is definitely one for the album!

blancmange

1 tablespoon cornflour
2/3 cup (160ml) formula or breast milk
2 teaspoons sugar
1/4 teaspoon vanilla essence

Blend cornflour with 1 tablespoon of the milk in a small bowl until smooth. Bring remaining milk to boil in small pan; remove from heat. Add sugar, vanilla and cornflour mixture, stirring over heat until mixture boils and thickens. Pour blancmange into small bowl, cover; refrigerate several hours or until set.

MAKES 2/3 CUP (160ml)

Storage Covered, in refrigerator, up to 2 days

apricot puree with blended rice cereal

2/3 cup (100g) dried apricots
1 1/2 cups (375ml) water
2 tablespoons blended cereal
1/3 cup (80ml) formula or breast milk, warmed

Combine apricots and water in small pan; simmer, covered, about 20 minutes or until apricots are tender. Blend apricots and cooking liquid until smooth.

Mix cereal in small bowl with breast milk or formula; serve topped with 1 tablespoon apricot puree.

PUREE MAKES 1 1/4 CUPS (310ml)

Storage Puree, covered, in refrigerator up to 2 days
Freeze Puree, suitable in individual portions

APRICOT PUREE WITH BLENDED RICE CEREAL

food intolerance As a small number of babies find it difficult to digest **gluten** (found in wheat products), it's best to avoid this in the first 6 months. That's why we start with rice cereal – although soy, maize, sago and tapioca are also suitable. **Egg white** can also occasionally cause an adverse reaction so it's best to avoid eggs until 9 to 12 months.

apple semolina

3 teaspoons semolina
1/3 cup (80ml) cooled boiled water
1/3 cup (80ml) apple juice

Combine all ingredients in small pan; simmer, uncovered, about 2 minutes or until thickened slightly.

MAKES 2/3 CUP (160ml)

Storage Covered, in refrigerator, up to 2 days

APPLE SEMOLINA

ricotta with pear puree

1/3 cup (65g) ricotta cheese
2 tablespoons pureed pear

Push cheese through a fine sieve. Mix cheese in small bowl with pureed pear until smooth. Add a little extra breast milk or cooled boiled water if necessary.

MAKES 1/2 CUP (125ml)

Storage Covered, in refrigerator, up to 2 days

RICOTTA WITH PEAR PUREE

PREPARED BABY FOODS

Commercial baby foods are useful "convenience" foods when travelling or in an emergency, and can be used on their own or in conjunction with homemade foods. They are quick to prepare, safe and the range is extensive; however, they are often less economical than the foods you make yourself and tend to provide less variety in texture and taste.

• Always check labels before purchasing commercial baby foods so that you are fully aware of their contents.

• Discard any remaining portions of commercial baby food if your child has been fed directly from the container.

• If you know beforehand that all the food will not be eaten, spoon a single serving from the container and heat it separately. The remaining food, covered tightly, can be refrigerated for up to 2 days.

• Commercial baby food in glass jars can be reheated in a saucepan half-filled with boiling water or placed in your microwave oven – but always remember to remove a jar's metal lid though before reheating in a microwave.

6 to 9 months
TASTE TESTING

This is when eating starts to become much more fun – and a whole lot messier as well!

Your baby now sits happily in the high chair and actually anticipates his mealtimes. He might not be bored with cereal and fruit, but you probably are, and now that he's eating confidently, it's time to widen his culinary experience with lots more tastes and textures.

Once again, remember to be flexible as you introduce new foods. Baby is quite possibly not going to like every single thing you offer – after all, *you* like some foods more than others. You might also find, as you begin to add foods with a little more texture, that babies who happily scoffed a velvety puree will be deeply insulted by the merest suggestion of a lump. Don't force the issue, just proceed slowly and remember that by offering as wide a variety as possible, you're more likely to be providing a "balanced diet" without needing to become obsessed with food charts.

Unless your early childhood nurse advises otherwise, you should now start to offer the food *before* the milk – the opposite to what you have been doing until now, as baby is gradually going to get more and more nourishment from solids rather than milk.

porridge

Best made just before mealtime, porridge can be served with warm or cold milk, a little golden syrup or pureed fruit.

1/3 cup (30g) rolled oats
3/4 cup (180ml) water or milk

Combine all ingredients in small pan; bring to boil, cook, stirring, about 2 minutes or until thickened.
MAKES 1 CUP (250ml)

Microwave Combine ingredients in microwave-safe jug, cover; microwave on HIGH (100%) about 2 minutes or until thickened, pausing halfway during cooking time to stir.

PORRIDGE

breakfast biscuits

Crush whole-wheat malted breakfast biscuits (such as Weet-bix, Shredded Wheat, etc.) with enough breast milk, formula or cooled boiled water until of desired consistency.

toast fingers

A great food for babies to suck and "chew". Toasted crusts are good, too.

blended rice cereal combo

Try stirring pureed fruit and yogurt into blended rice cereal.

TOAST FINGERS

BREAKFAST BISCUITS

Iron and your baby

From about 6 months of age, babies start to require extra iron in their diet. This is easily included if you plan to feed your baby meat, but for non meat-eating families, it can be a little more of a challenge.

Iron is present in some of the food that most babies eat (leafy greens, egg yolks, cereals, breads, beans and lentils, for instance); however, some of this iron is in a form not easily absorbed into the system.

If foods containing Vitamin C (citrus fruits, kiwi fruit, rockmelon, tomatoes, broccoli, pawpaw and capsicum) are consumed in conjunction with the foods listed earlier, absorption will be facilitated.

BLENDED RICE CEREAL COMBO

pureed mixed vegetables

Sweet potato, beans, broccoli or spinach can also be used. We've used this recipe in the others shown on this page.

1 medium (200g) potato, chopped coarsely
1 medium (120g) carrot, chopped coarsely
1 medium (120g) zucchini, chopped coarsely

Boil, steam or microwave vegetables until tender, drain; blend or process until smooth. If necessary, stir in a little breast milk, formula or cooled boiled water until of desired consistency.

MAKES 2 CUPS (500ml)

Storage Covered, in refrigerator, up to 2 days

Freeze Suitable, in individual portions

PUREED MIXED VEGETABLES
WITH FRIED LAMB PUREE

white or cheese sauce

Try both versions of this sauce with pureed mixed vegetables to introduce new tastes to your baby.

20g butter
2 teaspoons plain flour
1/2 cup (125ml) formula or breast milk
1 tablespoon finely grated cheddar cheese, optional

Melt butter in small pan. Stir in flour; cook, stirring, until bubbling. Remove from heat; gradually stir in milk. Cook, stirring, until mixture boils and thickens; add cheese, if using. Stir sauce through pureed vegetables.

MAKES 1/2 CUP (125ml)

Storage Covered, in refrigerator, up to 2 days

CHEESE SAUCE

steamed fish puree

1 small (150g) fish fillet

Remove any bones or skin from fish. Place in steamer basket; cook, covered, over pan of simmering water about 5 minutes or until cooked through.
Blend or process with a little breast milk, formula or cooled boiled water until of desired consistency. Serve with pureed green vegetables.

MAKES ABOUT 1/2 CUP (125ml)

Storage Covered, in refrigerator, up to 2 days

Freeze Suitable, in individual portions

fried lamb puree

Any lean lamb, from a small fillet or trimmed from a leg, or lean beef can be used for this recipe.

1/2 teaspoon olive oil
1 lamb cutlet, trimmed

Heat oil in small pan, cook lamb until browned both sides and cooked through. When cool enough to handle, remove meat from bone; blend or process with a little breast milk, formula or cooled boiled water until smooth. Serve with pureed vegetables, if desired.

MAKES 1/4 CUP (60ml)

Storage Covered, in refrigerator up to 2 days

Freeze Suitable, in individual portions

STEAMED FISH PUREE WITH
PUREED GREEN VEGETABLES

chicken stock

Omit the chicken and you'll have a healthy and tasty vegetable stock good for soups and sauces, or for thinning purees.

500g chicken bones
3 trimmed (225g) celery sticks, chopped
2 medium (250g) carrots, chopped
1 medium (150g) brown onion, chopped
1 sprig parsley
1 bay leaf
2 litres (8 cups) water

Combine all ingredients in large pan; simmer, uncovered, 1 hour. Strain into large bowl; discard bones and vegetables. Refrigerate stock overnight. Remove and discard solidified fat from the surface. If stock is to be kept longer, it is best to freeze it in small quantities. When reheating stock, be sure to bring it to the boil before using.

MAKES 6 CUPS (1.5 litres)

Storage Covered, in refrigerator, up to 2 days
Freeze Suitable, in individual portions

☺TIP Great finger food A cooked and cooled lamb cutlet bone makes a great treat for an older baby to suck and "chew" on.

chicken and vegetable soup

2 (440g) chicken thighs
1 litre (4 cups) chicken stock (at left)
1 small (80g) brown onion, chopped
1 medium (120g) carrot, chopped
1 trimmed (75g) celery stick, chopped
1 small (120g) potato, chopped
2 tablespoons barley

CHICKEN AND VEGETABLE SOUP

Remove fat from chicken. Place chicken and stock in medium pan, bring to boil; simmer, uncovered, 30 minutes. Strain over large bowl; reserve chicken and cooking liquid. Remove meat from chicken thighs; discard bones. Return chicken, liquid, vegetables and barley to same pan; simmer, uncovered, about 15 minutes or until barley is tender. Blend or process, in batches, until just smooth.

MAKES 4 CUPS (1 litre)

Storage Covered, in refrigerator, up to 2 days
Freeze Suitable, in individual portions
Rice or pasta can be substituted for barley in this recipe.

POTATO SOUP

potato soup

3 medium (600g) potatoes, chopped
3 cups (750ml) chicken (or vegetable) stock

Place potatoes in medium pan with stock; bring to boil. Simmer, covered, about 15 minutes or until potatoes are tender. Blend or process, in batches, until smooth. Serve, topped with toast cubes for older babies, if desired.

MAKES 4 CUPS (1 litre)

Storage Covered, in refrigerator, up to 2 days. Reheat as required, thinning if necessary with a little stock, formula or breast milk
Freeze Suitable, in individual portions

CHICKEN STOCK

lamb shank broth

1 lamb shank, trimmed
1 medium (200g) potato, chopped coarsely
1 medium (120g) carrot, chopped coarsely
1 trimmed (75g) celery stick, chopped coarsely
1 tablespoon barley
1 litre (4 cups) water

Place all ingredients in medium pan; bring to boil. Simmer, covered, about 1 hour or until meat is tender. When cool enough to handle, remove lamb shank from pan; remove meat from shank, discard bone. Blend or process meat with vegetables and cooking liquid, in batches, until soup is almost smooth.

MAKES 4 CUPS (1 litre)

Storage Covered, in refrigerator, up to 2 days
Freeze Suitable, in individual portions

LAMB SHANK BROTH

foods to avoid at this stage

Because they've been known to cause adverse reactions in a small number of babies, honey, peanut products and strawberries should all be avoided until baby is at least 12 months old. Egg white should also be delayed until 9 to 12 months.

zucchini and corn pasta

Elbow macaroni or orzo can be substituted for risoni.

20g butter
1 small (50g) tomato, chopped finely
1 small (90g) zucchini, grated coarsely
1/3 cup (60g) risoni
2 tablespoons creamed corn

Melt butter in small pan; cook tomato and zucchini, stirring, until vegetables are tender. Meanwhile, cook risoni in medium pan of boiling water, uncovered, until tender; drain. Combine warm risoni and vegetable mixture with corn in small bowl.

MAKES ABOUT 2 CUPS (500ml)

Storage Covered, in refrigerator, up to 2 days
Freeze Suitable, in individual portions

ZUCCHINI AND CORN PASTA

stewed fruit compote

2 cups (500ml) water
1/3 cup (50g) dried apricots
1/3 cup (55g) seeded prunes
1 small (180g) pear, peeled, quartered, sliced thickly
1 cinnamon stick
1 tablespoon brown sugar

Combine all ingredients in medium pan; simmer, covered, about 20 minutes or until pears are tender. Cool; discard cinnamon stick. Serve mashed, with yogurt, if desired.

MAKES ABOUT 2 CUPS (500ml)

Storage Covered, in refrigerator, up to 2 days
Freeze Suitable, in individual portions

STEWED FRUIT COMPOTE

fruit jelly

2 cups (500ml) fruit juice
3 teaspoons powdered gelatine

Place 1/4 cup of the juice in a cup; sprinkle gelatine over juice. Stand cup in small pan of simmering water, stir until gelatine is dissolved. Stir gelatine mixture into remaining juice in medium bowl; refrigerate until firm.

FRUIT JELLY

daily meal plan

This plan only includes 3 breast- or bottle-feeds. Quite often young babies are still on 4 or 5 milk feeds, so continue with these feeds within this plan in a way that suits you and your baby. Lunch and dinner suggestions are interchangeable. Times are merely a guide.

EARLY MORNING
6am   Breast or bottle

BREAKFAST
8am   Porridge or Weet-bix
       Toast fingers
       Diluted juice

MORNING TEA
10am   Yogurt and fruit
       Water/diluted juice

LUNCH
12.30pm Creamy
vegetable
  puree
       Breast or bottle

AFTERNOON TEA
3pm   Mashed banana
       Water/diluted juice

DINNER
5.30pm Lamb shank broth
       Fruit Jelly
       Breast or bottle

9 to 12 months
GREATER VARIETY

The greatest change around now is that your baby probably has teeth, making finger food a new option. But don't think that a lack of teeth means she can't have finger food – her little gums are hard enough to deal with a variety of foods. Your baby will probably love finger food – not only does it offer a whole new range of interesting tastes and textures, it also gives her a measure of control that appeals to her newly developing sense of independence. You'll also find that finger food provides a marvellous distraction from playing pat-a-cake with the rest of her meal. At this stage, it is only going to be a temporary distraction and despite the fact that mealtimes can end with both of you looking as though you've been rolling in the dish of the day, it's important to let your baby experiment with her food. Those inquisitive little fingers will eventually transfer some of the meal into her mouth! Her enthusiasm is more important than your kitchen floor – if she wants to have the spoon, give her one of her own; this is the first step to learning to feed herself, after all.

Helping fussy eaters to eat

Some babies can be very contrary when it comes to food, even those who started as textbook eaters. Try not to worry if food is refused – your baby is not going to starve! He may simply have begun to work out that his refusal to eat produces interesting results – lots of attention, for a start.

• Don't allow babies to eat or drink too much between mealtimes – this can lead to refusing meals. On the other hand, if the small-and-often form of eating is mutually acceptable, food eaten as a snack is just as nutritious as the same food eaten at specific "mealtimes".

• Experiment with different flavours, textures and combinations, but don't impose *your* idea of a suitable combination on the baby – if he wants to dip a chop bone in his bread and butter pudding, then who cares?

• If your fussy eater will only eat one favourite food, there is nothing wrong with serving it up repeatedly. Offer alternatives but don't get upset if they're refused.

• Try to keep it a happy time (no matter how stressed you feel) – a story or song can occasionally help, but don't feel you have to put on *Showboat* either, or draw faces or fly aeroplanes with every mouthful: it's not dinner and a show! Allow the meal to end when he indicates he has had enough and resist the temptation to turn cartwheels in order to encourage a few last mouthfuls. It's a rare child who won't grasp the opportunity to see you do it again and again, then demand somersaults as well!

muesli

We used dried apples, apricots and currants in this version but try experimenting with raisins, dried peaches or dates to find your baby's particular likes and dislikes.

1 breakfast biscuit, crushed
¼ cup (10g) bran flakes
¼ cup (10g) rice bubbles
½ cup (75g) your choice dried fruit, chopped finely
2 teaspoons desiccated coconut

Combine all ingredients in medium bowl. Serve with formula, breast milk or yogurt and chopped fresh fruit, if desired.

MAKES 1½ CUPS

Storage Airtight container, up to 1 week

MUESLI

pikelets

1 cup (150g) self-raising flour
2 tablespoons caster sugar
1 egg, beaten lightly
¾ cup (180ml) milk, approximately

Combine flour and sugar in medium bowl; gradually whisk in egg and enough milk to make a thick, smooth batter. Drop dessertspoons of mixture into greased heavy-base pan; cook until bubbles begin to appear on surface of pikelet, turn, brown other side. Serve with yogurt and a little stewed or pureed fruit, if desired, or a drizzle of maple syrup.

MAKES ABOUT 20

Storage Airtight container, up to 2 days

PIKELETS

homemade rusks

1 loaf unsliced bread

Trim crusts from all sides and ends of loaf. Cut bread into 1.5cm slices; cut slices into 1.5cm-thick fingers. Place on oven trays, bake in very slow oven about 1 hour or until bread is dried and crisp.

MAKES ABOUT 70

Storage Airtight container, up to 1 week

From 9 months, baby can have cow's milk in cooking, unless your doctor or early childhood nurse advises otherwise.

fruit muffins

2 cups (300g) self-raising flour
1 teaspoon mixed spice
½ cup (100g) firmly packed brown sugar
½ cup (80g) sultanas
1 cup (250ml) milk
125g butter, melted
1 egg, beaten lightly

Grease three 12-hole small (2-tablespoon/40ml-capacity) muffin pans. Combine flour, spice, sugar and sultanas in large bowl. Stir in milk, butter and egg; do not overmix (batter should be coarse and slightly lumpy). Divide mixture among pan holes; bake muffins in moderately hot oven about 15 minutes or until browned.

MAKES 36

Storage Airtight container, up to 2 days
Freeze Suitable

FRUIT MUFFINS

☺TIP Vary the flavour of these muffins by changing the dried fruit to either chopped dried apricots, raisins, seeded dates or seeded prunes, or a combination of any of these.

SCRAMBLED EGG

scrambled egg

1 egg
1 tablespoon milk
1 teaspoon butter

Whisk egg and milk in small bowl. Heat butter in small pan, add egg mixture; cook over low heat, stirring gently, until egg just sets. Serve with buttered bread.

☺TIP Make scrambled egg just before serving. Remember that this cannot be fed to children who have not yet successfully included egg in their diet.

POACHED EGG

poached egg

Break 1 egg into small shallow pan of gently simmering water; turn off heat, place lid on pan; stand about 3 minutes or until egg white is just set. Remove with slotted spoon or egg slide, serve immediately.

avocado dip

1/2 ripe avocado
1/4 cup (30g) finely grated cheddar cheese
1 tablespoon finely chopped tomato
1 teaspoon yogurt

Blend, process or mash all ingredients in small bowl. Serve with blanched vegetable sticks for older children or as a meal for younger babies.

MAKES 1/2 CUP (125ml)
Best made just before serving

daily meal plan

EARLY MORNING
6am   Breast or bottle

BREAKFAST
8am   Muesli
        Toast fingers
        Diluted juice

MORNING TEA
10am   Muffin
        Water/diluted juice

LUNCH
12.30pm Chopped
tomato
        and bread
        Breast or bottle

AFTERNOON TEA
3pm   Mashed banana
        Water/diluted juice

DINNER
5.30pm Chicken and
        vegetable soup
        Egg custard
        Breast
        or bottle

chopped tomato and bread

A delicious light meal for an older baby. Toss chopped buttered bread, crusts removed, with chopped skinned and seeded tomato in small bowl; add a little grated cheese, cottage cheese or chopped ham, as desired.

CHOPPED TOMATO AND BREAD
WITH AVOCADO DIP

bread and butter pudding

2 slices white bread, crusts removed
butter
1 1/4 cups (310ml) milk
2 eggs
1 tablespoon caster sugar
1/4 teaspoon vanilla essence
pinch ground nutmeg

Spread bread lightly with butter; cut into small triangle-shaped pieces. Divide bread among four 1/2 cup (125ml) greased heatproof dishes; place dishes in baking dish. Whisk milk, eggs, sugar and vanilla in medium jug; pour egg mixture over bread, sprinkle with nutmeg. Pour enough boiling water into baking dish to come halfway up sides of dishes. Bake, uncovered, in moderate oven about 20 minutes or until puddings are just set.

MAKES 4 SERVINGS

Storage Covered, in refrigerator, up to 2 days

☺TIP **Stirred custard** You can make a plain stirred custard easily by beating the same quantities of eggs and sugar shown above together, in the top half of a double saucepan or small heatproof bowl, until mixture starts to thicken, then whisking in the same amounts of warmed milk and vanilla. Place pan or bowl over top of a larger pan half-filled with simmering water; cook, stirring, until custard is thick enough to coat the back of a spoon. Be careful not to overheat the custard or allow water to touch base of pan as custard could curdle. Remove from heat and larger pan as soon as the custard has thickened.

BREAD AND BUTTER PUDDING

quick creamed rice

1/2 cup (125ml) milk
2 teaspoons brown sugar
1/4 cup cooked calrose rice

Combine milk and sugar in small pan; bring to boil, stir in rice. Cook, stirring, about 5 minutes or until thickened. Serve topped with fruit, if desired.

MAKES 1 SERVING

Storage Covered, in refrigerator, up to 2 days

QUICK CREAMED RICE

sweet couscous

3/4 cup (180ml) milk
1 tablespoon couscous
1 teaspoon sugar
pinch ground cinnamon

Combine all ingredients in small pan; simmer, stirring, about 12 minutes or until thickened.
Serve with sliced banana, if desired.

MAKES 1 SERVING

Storage Covered, in refrigerator, up to 2 days

SWEET COUSCOUS

12 to 18 months
BITE-SIZE BITS

By the beginning of the second year, your toddler will probably be ready to share quite a number of the foods you serve to the rest of the family – the goal is in sight! However, all children vary in their development. At this age, some are adventurous with their tastes while others are totally uninterested in the whole business. Some will only eat if they can feed themselves, while others still absolutely insist on being spoon-fed every mouthful. This shouldn't really come as a surprise – just like adults, children's tastes and the size of their appetites vary with each individual.

That's why our menus are only guidelines, not rules, and flexibility is still the key to retaining your sanity and sense of humour. If your toddler thinks scrambled eggs are beyond the pale, whip the egg into a custard instead – it has the same nutritional value.

Children who are already walking will tend to use up more energy and might be hungrier than their less-mobile counterparts. If your child is at the stage where she needs extra food and is feeding herself quite competently – taking bite-size pieces, then chewing and swallowing before putting more in her mouth – you can now introduce more advanced meals.

For those babies whose tastes are still rather conservative, you will need to proceed slowly as you add new tastes and textures. It is important however, to foster independence – instead of simply spooning the food into her mouth, place a filled spoon in her hand and let her take it to her mouth herself. This reinforces the idea that she is the one making the decisions about eating and with all the magnificent perversity of the one-year-old mind, this might help to make her more adventurous about what she eats!

MINI LENTIL PATTIES

filled baby potatoes

A quick and tasty meal for young toddlers. Bake, boil, steam or microwave tiny new potatoes until tender; drain. Halve potatoes; scoop out a third of the flesh then trim bases so they sit flat. Combine potato flesh with a filling of your choice and spoon into potatoes. Try your toddler with some of the following flavours:

- mashed boiled egg mixed with a dollop of low-fat mayonnaise
- mashed avocado with finely chopped ham
- baked beans

AVOCADO AND HAM

BOILED EGG AND MAYONNAISE

BAKED BEANS

mini lentil patties

1/4 cup (50g) red lentils
200g coarsely chopped kumara
**2 tablespoons finely
    chopped celery**
1/4 cup coarsely grated apple
1/2 clove garlic, crushed
1/4 cup (15g) stale breadcrumbs
**1/2 cup (50g) packaged
    breadcrumbs**

Add lentils to small pan of boiling water; boil, uncovered, about 10 minutes or until tender; drain. Meanwhile, boil, steam or microwave kumara until tender; drain, mash until smooth.

Combine lentils and kumara in small bowl with celery, apple, garlic and breadcrumbs; shape tablespoons of mixture into patties. Coat patties in packaged breadcrumbs; place on oiled oven tray, spray lightly with cooking-oil spray. Bake in moderate oven 15 minutes or until patties are browned lightly.

MAKES 16 PATTIES

Storage Covered, in refrigerator, up to 2 days
Freeze Suitable

SAFETY TIP Babies should be supervised at all times with finger food. Because of the choking hazard, do not give children under 5 years whole nuts or other small, hard pieces of food.

spinach and ricotta ravioli with buttered crumbs

Introduce various other filled pastas to your toddler.

**2/3 cup (90g) ravioli filled with
    spinach and ricotta**
10g butter
1/4 cup (15g) stale breadcrumbs

Add ravioli to medium pan of boiling water; boil, uncovered, until tender; drain. Meanwhile, melt butter in small pan, add breadcrumbs; cook, stirring, until browned lightly. Toss breadcrumbs through ravioli.

MAKES 1 SERVING

Best made just before serving

SPINACH AND RICOTTA RAVIOLI WITH BUTTERED CRUMBS

daily meal plan

EARLY MORNING
6am   Breast or milk

BREAKFAST
8am   Scrambled egg
with toast fingers
Fresh fruit or juice

MORNING TEA
10am   Yogurt or cheese
snack

LUNCH
12.30pm Corn and broccoli
florets
Breast or bottle

AFTERNOON TEA
3pm   Banana fruit ice
Water/juice

DINNER
5.30pm   Mini lentil patties
with chopped tomato
and avocado
Jelly
Breast or bottle

SAUSAGES WITH VEGETABLES AND GRAVY

CORN AND BROCCOLI FLORETS

sausages with vegetables and gravy

2 (160g) thin beef sausages
1/4 cup (30g) frozen peas
4 (30g) baby carrots
1 medium (200g) potato, chopped coarsely
1 teaspoon butter
2 tablespoons milk
2 teaspoons Gravox
1/2 cup (125ml) water

Cook sausages on heated oiled griddle pan (or grill or barbecue) until browned all over and cooked as desired; cover to keep warm.

Boil, steam or microwave vegetables, separately, until tender; drain. Mash potatoes with butter and milk until smooth. Combine Gravox and water in small pan; cook, stirring, until gravy boils and thickens. Simmer, uncovered, 2 minutes.

MAKES 2 SERVINGS

Storage Covered, separately, in refrigerator, up to 2 days
Freeze Uncooked sausages suitable

corn and broccoli florets

1 bacon rasher, chopped finely
130g can creamed corn
1 cup (85g) broccoli florets

Heat medium pan; cook bacon, stirring, until crisp, drain on absorbent paper.

Heat corn in medium pan; add bacon, cook until hot.

Boil, steam or microwave broccoli until tender; drain. Place corn and bacon mixture in centre of plate; arrange broccoli around corn.

MAKES 2 SERVINGS

Storage Covered, in refrigerator, up to 2 days

PASTA SHELLS WITH CHOPPED HAM, AVOCADO AND TOMATO

pasta shells

Toss pre-cooked pasta shells or other pasta shapes with a combination of any or all of the following, served warm or cold: cottage cheese, grated cheese, chopped tomato, chopped avocado or chopped ham. This makes delicious fingerfood even though a tad messy!

jelly

Use a packet of jelly to prepare an all-time favourite – just follow the manufacturer's instructions. Alternatively, use fresh fruit juice in place of the water, and stir in freshly chopped fruit (avoid pineapple as it prevents jelly from setting).

banana fruit ice

This is a deliciously healthy ice-cream substitute that can be served as a snack or dessert.

Mash 1 ripe medium (200g) banana in small bowl; divide banana between two small freezer-safe containers. Cover; freeze several hours or overnight. Just before serving, remove from freezer; stand 5 minutes. Using a fork, beat banana until light-coloured and creamy.

MAKES 2 SERVINGS

JELLY

BANANA FRUIT ICE

2to3 years
QUICK AND EASY MEALS

Anyone who has had a close encounter with a two-year-old knows that occasionally it is well nigh impossible to avoid losing your cool at mealtimes. On the one hand, you have a little person who is now able to eat almost anything the rest of the family eats, as well as feed himself with a considerable degree of dexterity. On the other hand, you have the average two-year-old — quixotic, wilful, capricious and alert to even the slightest signal that this eating business might matter to you. Don't be drawn into the game — if food is refused, remove it without a fuss.

It might sound silly, but try to think like a two-year-old. She is insatiably curious and loves to "help". Find a small, safe task that will involve the child in the meal preparation. If she has had a hand in the preparation, she might be more inclined to eat it.

Piling large amounts of food onto the plate can also be very off-putting — just think what it must look like! Keep the serving toddler-sized and arrange it attractively — you know yourself how important presentation can be to your enjoyment of a meal. You don't have to go to the trouble of making a funny face out of everything you serve, but keep it varied and appealing . . . and small.

Serve food that you know your child enjoys. Don't worry if it's almost the same meal every night — it doesn't matter. Try to find substitutes for food that is disliked rather than having a battle of wills over the hated item. For instance, if she loathes vegies, serve more fruit; if milk offends, try cheese or yogurt; if he hates chewing meat, offer protein that is easier to chew, such as mince, chicken or fish.

And on the days when you're starting to feel completely outwitted, keep reminding yourself that you're grown-up and your toddler is not!

frankfurt and beans

**1 (90g) continental frankfurt,
   chopped coarsely**
130g can baked beans
**1 medium (190g) tomato,
   chopped finely**
1 mushroom, chopped finely
2 tablespoons chopped red capsicum
¼ cup (60ml) milk

Combine all ingredients in small pan; bring
to boil. Simmer, uncovered, until mixture
thickens slightly. Serve with crusty bread
or toast fingers.

MAKES 2 SERVINGS

Storage Covered, in refrigerator, up to 2 days
Freeze Suitable, in portion sizes

FRANKFURT AND BEANS

beef 'n' vegie patties

250g minced beef
**1 small (70g) carrot,
   grated coarsely**
**1 small (90g) zucchini,
   grated coarsely**
**1 small (120g) potato,
   grated coarsely**
**½ small (40g) onion,
   chopped finely**
1 tablespoon tomato sauce
1 egg, beaten lightly
vegetable oil, for shallow frying

Using hand, combine beef, carrot, zucchini, potato,
onion, sauce and egg in large bowl; shape
tablespoons of mixture into patties. Heat oil in
medium pan; shallow-fry patties, in batches, until
browned both sides and cooked through. Drain
patties on absorbent paper; serve with noodles
or rice, if desired.

MAKES ABOUT 20

Storage Uncooked mixture can be kept, covered, in
refrigerator up to a day ahead
Freeze Suitable, uncooked, in individual portions

☺TIP This mixture also makes a tasty meatloaf;
press in an oiled 8cm x 26cm bar cake pan and bake
in moderate oven about 45 minutes or until firm and
cooked through.

BEEF 'N' VEGIE PATTIES

fish croquettes

1 medium (200g) potato
105g can salmon, drained
1 egg, beaten lightly
2 tablespoons finely grated carrot
2 tablespoons finely grated zucchini
2 tablespoons finely grated cheddar cheese
2 tablespoons plain flour
2 teaspoons olive oil

Boil, steam or microwave potato until tender; drain. Mash in small bowl; allow to cool. Meanwhile, remove and discard bones from salmon; combine salmon, egg, carrot, zucchini and cheese with potato. Using rounded tablespoons of mixture, shape into croquettes. Toss in flour, shake away excess. Heat oil in small non-stick pan; cook croquettes, in batches, until browned all over. Drain on absorbent paper; serve with lemon and tomato wedges and crustless bread.

MAKES 2 SERVINGS

Storage Uncooked mixture can be kept, covered, in refrigerator up to a day

Freeze Suitable, uncooked, in individual portions

☺TIP You can substitute canned tuna or steamed flaked fish fillet (be sure to remove any bones) for the salmon.

FISH CROQUETTES

pizza fingers

16cm x 20cm piece focaccia
$2/3$ cup (160ml) bottled tomato pasta sauce
1 medium (190g) tomato, halved, sliced
1 small (150g) red capsicum, chopped finely
60g mushrooms, sliced thinly
$1/2$ cup (85g) chopped ham
$1/2$ cup (110g) drained pineapple pieces
1 cup (125g) coarsely grated cheddar cheese
1 cup (100g) grated mozzarella cheese

Split bread in half horizontally. Place bread, split-side up, on oiled oven trays; spread with sauce. Top with remaining ingredients; bake in moderate oven about 15 minutes or until browned lightly. Cut into fingers to serve.

MAKES 2 TO 4 SERVINGS

Must be made just before serving

☺TIP You can also use cooked minced beef or other cooked chopped meat as part of the topping, if you desire. English muffins or a French stick, both halved through the centre, can be used for the pizza base.

PIZZA FINGERS

HAMBURGER WEDGES

hamburger wedges

250g minced beef

1/2 cup (35g) stale breadcrumbs

1 egg, beaten lightly

2 tablespoons fruit chutney

**1 tablespoon finely chopped
fresh parsley**

2 teaspoons olive oil

2 cheese slices

2 pieces pocket pitta bread

2 tablespoons tomato sauce

Combine beef, breadcrumbs, egg, chutney
and parsley in medium bowl; shape into
2 patties. Heat oil in medium pan; cook
patties until browned both sides and
cooked through. Place cheese on top of
patties during last 5 minutes of cooking.
Split pitta in half, spread each base-side
with sauce; top with patties and remaining
pitta. Cut into wedges, serve with salad
and crisp potato wedges.

MAKES 2 TO 4 SERVINGS

Storage Uncooked mixture can be kept,
covered, in refrigerator up to a day
Freeze Suitable, uncooked, in
individual portions

☺TIP To prepare potato wedges, scrub
4 small potatoes; dry with absorbent paper;
cut into wedges. Place wedges on oiled
oven tray, brush all over with olive oil.
Bake, uncovered, in hot oven about
45 minutes or until browned.

MACARONI CHEESE (LEFT) WITH BEEF AND VEGETABLE RICE

macaroni cheese

We used 1/2 cup (75g) uncooked short macaroni, but you can use elbow macaroni or even small pasta shells if you wish.

30g butter
1 tablespoon plain flour
1 cup (250ml) milk
1/2 cup (60g) coarsely grated cheddar cheese
1 1/3 cups cooked macaroni

Heat butter in small pan, add flour; cook, stirring, until mixture thickens and bubbles. Gradually stir in milk; stir until mixture boils and thickens. Add cheese and macaroni; stir over heat until cheese melts and mixture is heated through.
Top with chopped tomato, if desired.

MAKES 1 SERVING

Storage Covered, in refrigerator, up to 2 days

☺TIP Place macaroni mixture in small oiled ovenproof dish; top with small amounts of finely chopped crisped bacon, chopped tomato, extra grated cheddar cheese and fresh breadcrumbs. Bake in moderate oven about 10 minutes or until browned lightly.

beef and vegetable rice

About 2 1/2 tablespoons of uncooked calrose rice makes the 1/2 cup cooked rice you need for this recipe.

2 teaspoons olive oil
60g minced beef
1 medium (190g) egg tomato, chopped finely
1 mushroom, chopped finely
1/4 cup (30g) frozen peas
1/2 cup cooked calrose rice
1/4 cup (30g) coarsely grated cheddar cheese

Heat oil in small pan; cook beef, stirring, until browned. Add tomato, mushroom and peas; cook, stirring, until vegetables soften. Stir in rice; sprinkle with cheese.

MAKES 1 SERVING

Storage Covered, in refrigerator, up to 2 days
Freeze Suitable, in individual portions

☺TIP Try adapting this recipe to make fried rice. Simply cook small amounts of finely chopped ham, green onions and drained canned corn kernels in medium pan; stir in cooked rice with a little soy sauce. You can also mix leftover vegetables or casseroles with cooked rice for a toddler's meal.

fish 'n' chips

1/4 cup (40g) plain flour
1 tablespoon milk
2 tablespoons water
1 medium (200g) potato
vegetable oil, for deep frying
125g boneless white fish fillet

Place flour in small bowl, gradually whisk in combined milk and water; cover, stand batter 10 minutes. Cut potatoes into 1cm slices; cut slices into 1cm strips. Rinse potato chips under cold water, drain; dry with absorbent paper. Deep-fry chips in hot oil until browned lightly; drain on absorbent paper. Meanwhile, remove and discard any skin or bones from fish; cut fish into bite-size pieces. Dip fish in batter, drain off excess. Deep-fry fish, in batches, until browned and cooked through; drain on absorbent paper. Serve with mayonnaise for dipping, if desired, with salad and crusty bread.

MAKES 1 SERVING

Best made just before serving

difficult though it sometimes may be try not to elevate sweet food to treat or reward status. It's very tempting to say, "If you eat this enormous and unappetising plate of boiled spinach, then you can have this wonderfully sweet pudding." Look at it from the child's point of view: you are clearly indicating that the pudding is much more desirable than the vegies. What two-year-old isn't going to hold out for the sweet stuff? He clamps his lips at the spinach, you refuse to serve the pudding and the battle is on! The solution? Serve a nutritious, low sugar dessert and if he wants to eat it first occasionally, the world won't come to a crashing halt.

MINESTRONE

425g can tomatoes
300g can four-bean mix, drained
1 cup (250ml) water
1/2 cup (75g) short tubular pasta
1/4 cup (30g) coarsely grated
    cheddar cheese

Heat oil in large pan; cook onion and bacon, stirring, until onion is soft. Add celery, carrot, potato and zucchini; cook, stirring, until vegetables have just softened. Stir in undrained crushed tomatoes, beans, water and pasta; simmer, covered, 20 minutes or until vegetables and pasta are tender. Serve topped with cheese and homemade croutons, if desired.

MAKES 4 TO 6 SERVINGS

Storage Covered, in refrigerator, up to 2 days
Freeze Suitable, in individual portions

☺TIP Toddlers love to be involved with their food: allow children to add their own cheese and croutons to the minestrone. Make croutons the quick and easy way by simply cutting toast into small cubes. Make more traditional croutons by baking crustless bread shapes in a moderate oven about 10 minutes, or by frying them in equal amounts of butter and oil until browned lightly; drain on absorbent paper.

FISH 'N' CHIPS

LEFTOVER ROAST DINNER CASSEROLE

vegie pies with rice crusts

You will need ²/₃ cup (130g) uncooked calrose rice for the pie crusts.

1¹/₂ cups cooked calrose rice

2 tablespoons finely grated parmesan cheese

1 egg yolk

FILLING

20g butter

50g button mushrooms, chopped finely

1 small (90g) zucchini, grated coarsely

¹/₂ small (60g) tomato, chopped finely

¹/₂ cup (100g) ricotta cheese

1 egg yolk

Oil deep 12-hole patty pan. Combine rice, cheese and egg yolk in small bowl; using wet hand, press 1 tablespoon of mixture over base of each hole in prepared pan. Spoon Filling into rice shells; bake in moderate oven about 25 minutes until Filling is set and rice crusts browned lightly.

leftover roast dinner casserole

30g butter

1 tablespoon plain flour

1 cup (250ml) milk

1 cup (120g) chopped cooked meat or chicken

1 cup (150g) chopped cooked vegetables

¹/₄ cup (15g) stale breadcrumbs

¹/₂ cup (75g) coarsely grated cheddar cheese

Heat butter in small pan, add flour; cook, stirring, until mixture thickens and bubbles. Gradually stir in milk; stir until mixture boils and thickens. Place combined meat and vegetables in shallow oiled 2-cup (500ml) ovenproof dish; pour sauce over the top. Sprinkle with combined breadcrumbs and cheese; bake, uncovered, in moderate oven about 20 minutes or until heated through and browned on top.

MAKES 2 TO 3 SERVINGS

Best made just before serving

easy as pie

Place leftover savoury mince, bolognese sauce, or a mild meat or vegetable curry in small greased ovenproof dishes; top with rounds of ready-rolled puff pastry. Brush pastry with milk; pierce tops to create vents. Bake in hot oven about 10 minutes or until heated through and browned on top.

SAVOURY MINCE TOPPED WITH PUFF PASTRY

VEGIE PIES WITH RICE CRUSTS

Filling Heat butter in small pan; cook mushrooms, zucchini and tomato, stirring, until vegetables are soft. Remove from heat; stir in ricotta and egg yolk.

MAKES 12

Storage Covered, in refrigerator, up to 2 days

Freeze Suitable, in individual portions

spreads for breads

Bread is one of life's great staples and the variety available these days
is nothing short of extraordinary, so there's no excuse for white bread boredom.
As well as your usual loaf, let your toddler try wholegrain, rye, fruit bread,
French bread sticks, crumpet fingers, English muffins, bagels, Turkish pide, lavash or
pitta bread and focaccia, to name but a few!

All of these breads can be topped or filled with any number of fillings that your
child enjoys – the combinations below are only the tip of the iceberg. Remember
too that this is a great way to disguise the vegetables and salads
that many toddlers try to avoid as their tastebuds become more selective.

FILLINGS AND TOPPINGS
cheese slices with tomato
mashed avocado and sprouts
devon, Berliner or any cold meat
cottage cheese and sultanas with honey
tuna, celery and mayonnaise
banana with peanut butter and honey
peanut butter with finely grated carrot and sultanas
anchovette

GRILLED TOPPINGS
ham, pineapple and cheese
baked beans and cheese
sweet corn or corn kernels
  with finely grated cheddar cheese
sardines and tomato sauce
cinnamon and sugar

The good egg

bacon and vegetable omelette

- **10g butter**
- **¹/₂ rasher bacon, chopped**
- **1 egg, beaten lightly**
- **1 teaspoon milk or water**
- **¹/₄ cup (40g) chopped cooked chicken**
- **1 tablespoon canned corn kernels**
- **1 tablespoon frozen peas, thawed, cooked**
- **¹/₄ cup (30g) coarsely grated cheddar cheese**

Heat butter in small non-stick pan; cook bacon, stirring, until crisp. Pour combined egg and milk into pan; cook, tilting pan, over medium heat until mixture starts to set. Sprinkle remaining ingredients over omelette, fold in half; cook, uncovered, about 1 minute or until heated through. When almost set, sprinkle with cheese, fold in half.

Serve with chopped tomato, lettuce and bread triangles, if desired.

MAKES 1 SERVING

Best made just before serving

FRENCH TOAST

BACON AND VEGETABLE OMELETTE

French toast

2 slices bread
1 egg
1 tablespoon milk
20g butter

Remove crust from bread; cut each slice into 4 triangles. Whisk egg and milk in small bowl. Heat butter in medium pan; dip triangles, one at a time, in egg mixture, cook until browned both sides. Serve drizzled with maple syrup, if desired.

MAKES 1 SERVING

Best made just before serving

egg florentine

20g butter
2 teaspoons plain flour
1/2 cup (125ml) milk
1/4 cup (30g) coarsely grated cheddar cheese
60g frozen spinach, thawed
1 egg
1 tablespoon coarsely grated cheddar cheese, extra

Heat butter in small pan, add flour; cook, stirring, until mixture thickens and bubbles. Gradually stir in milk; stir until mixture boils and thickens, stir in cheese. Using hand, squeeze spinach to extract as much liquid as possible; place spinach in oiled 1/2-cup (125ml) ovenproof dish. Press hollow in spinach with back of spoon; break egg over spinach, spoon sauce over spinach, sprinkle with extra cheese. Bake, uncovered, in moderate oven about 10 minutes or until egg is set.

MAKES 1 SERVING

Best made just before serving

SAVOURY SCRAMBLE

savoury scramble

20g butter
50g lean ham, chopped finely
2 small button mushrooms, chopped finely
1 tablespoon finely chopped tomato
1 egg, beaten lightly
1 tablespoon milk
2 tablespoons coarsely grated cheddar cheese

Heat butter in small pan; cook ham and mushrooms, stirring, until ham is browned. Stir in tomato and combined egg and milk; cook over low heat, stirring, until mixture starts to set. Stir in cheese; cook until mixture sets. Serve with buttered toast triangles.

MAKES 1 SERVING

Best made just before serving

EGG FLORENTINE

MEXI-MINCE

mexi-mince

2 teaspoons olive oil
125g minced beef
1/4 cup (60ml) beef stock
1 tablespoon tomato sauce
1 medium flour tortilla
1/4 cup finely shredded lettuce
1/4 cup finely chopped tomato
2 tablespoons finely grated cheddar cheese

Heat oil in small pan; cook beef, stirring, until browned through. Add stock; simmer, uncovered, about 5 minutes or until stock has almost evaporated. Cut tortilla into triangles; heat in moderately hot oven about 2 minutes or just until triangles begin to crisp. Serve beef mixture topped with lettuce, tomato, cheese and tortilla triangles.

MAKES 1 TO 2
SERVINGS

*Must be made
just before serving*

☺TIP Toddlers under three should be very strictly supervised with taco shells or corn chips.

when is a sandwich not a sandwich?

Jaffles are the answer to a busy mother's prayer. They are quick, nourishing, easy to handle and different enough from the usual sandwich to persuade a fussy eater to take a bite.

Cheese is always the most requested filling in a jaffle but it's easy to be more adventurous – within their crunchy sealed edges, jaffles can often provide a complete nutritional meal that your child will gladly eat in preference to a sit-down dinner.

To make a jaffle Spread two slices of bread with butter. Place your selected filling on the *unbuttered* side of one slice and top with remaining bread, buttered-side out. Place jaffle in a preheated electric sandwich maker or jaffle iron. Cook until browned; cool 10 minutes before serving as **filling will be very hot.** Serve with salad (optimistic perhaps, but always worth a try).

THE SUNDAY ROAST
Leftover roast, vegetables and gravy – remember to chop all solid ingredients into bite-size pieces

CHICKEN FANTASTIQUE
Chopped cooked chicken with finely grated carrot, chopped avocado, mayonnaise

HAWAIIAN WAVES
Lean ham, drained crushed pineapple, creamed corn

JAFFLE BOLOGNESE
Savoury mince and grated parmesan cheese

SALMON SUPREME
Canned flaked red salmon, chopped avocado, chopped tomato, cream cheese

NUTTY SURPRISE
Nutella, chopped dried apricots, ricotta cheese

...when it's a jaffle!

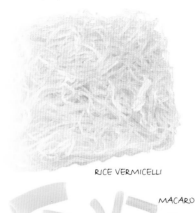

RICE VERMICELLI

MACARONI

RIGATONI

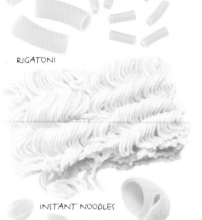

INSTANT NOODLES

SNAIL SHELLS

SMALL SHELLS

SPIRALS

PIPE RIGATE

EGG NOODLES

BOW-TIES

VERMICELLI

chicken 'n' noodles

¹/2 x 85g packet chicken-flavoured instant noodles
I cup (250ml) boiling water
I teaspoon vegetable oil
I green onion, chopped
I (110g) chicken thigh fillet, sliced thinly
3 snow peas, sliced thinly
3 green beans, sliced thinly
¹/4 cup sliced carrot
¹/4 cup sliced zucchini
2 teaspoons soy sauce

Combine noodles and boiling water in small bowl; stand 2 minutes. Stir in half of the flavour sachet; drain over small bowl, reserve ¹/4 cup (60ml) of the liquid. Heat oil in wok or medium pan; stir-fry chicken until browned and cooked through. Remove chicken from wok; cover to keep warm. Add vegetables to wok; stir-fry about 3 minutes or until just tender. Return chicken to wok with noodles, reserved liquid and soy sauce; stir-fry until heated through.

MAKES I SERVING

Best made just before serving

spring rolls

2 teaspoons olive oil
3 green onions, chopped finely
I small (70g) carrot, finely grated
I small (90g) zucchini, coarsely grated
³/4 cup (60g) finely shredded cabbage
¹/2 cup (20g) bean sprouts
125g minced lamb
³/4 cup (90g) coarsely grated cheddar cheese
12 sheets fillo pastry
¹/4 cup (60ml) olive oil, extra

Heat oil in wok or medium pan; stir-fry onion, carrot, zucchini, cabbage and sprouts 2 minutes. Add lamb, stir-fry until browned and cooked through. Remove from heat, stir in cheese; cool. Cover fillo with slightly damp tea-towel until ready to use to prevent its drying out. Remove I sheet fillo; brush with a little of the extra oil, fold in half lengthways then in half crossways. Fold again to form a IIcm x I4cm rectangle; brush with more oil. Place I rounded tablespoon of the filling mixture on each square; roll, folding in sides as you go. Brush lightly with oil; place on oiled oven tray. Repeat with remaining fillo and filling mixture. Bake in moderately hot oven about 15 minutes or until browned. Serve with sweet and sour or tomato sauce, if desired.

MAKES 12

Storage Uncooked mixture can be kept, covered, in refrigerator several hours ahead
Freeze Suitable, uncooked, individually

☺TIP Minced chicken can be substituted for lamb.

CHICKEN 'N' NOODLES

SALMON AND BROCCOLI PASTA

SPRING ROLLS

salmon and broccoli pasta

*We used bow-tie pasta (farfelle) but you can
use any sort of short pasta in this recipe.*

- **2 teaspoons butter**
- **I green onion, chopped finely**
- **2 tablespoons finely
  chopped broccoli**
- **I tablespoon water**
- **I tablespoon spreadable
  cream cheese**
- **I tablespoon drained canned
  red salmon**
- **¹/2 cup (45g) pasta**

Heat butter in small pan; cook onion,
broccoli and water, stirring, until broccoli
is tender. Add cream cheese; cook, stirring,
until melted. Stir in salmon. Meanwhile,
cook pasta in medium pan of boiling
water, uncovered, until just tender; drain.
Gently toss pasta in small bowl with
salmon mixture.

MAKES I SERVING
Best made just before serving.

QUICK-MIX ICE-CREAM

FRUIT SALAD

quick-mix ice-cream

600ml cream
400g can (300ml) condensed milk
1 teaspoon vanilla essence

Beat cream in small bowl with electric mixer until soft peaks form; gently fold in milk and vanilla. Pour mixture into deep 19cm square cake pan, cover with foil; freeze overnight or until firm.

MAKES 8 SERVINGS

☺TIP Fold through grated chocolate or pureed fruit before freezing ice-cream.

frozen yogurt

Puree 1/2 cup chopped fresh fruit of your choice; fold into 200g vanilla yogurt in small bowl. Pour into a freezer tray; freeze overnight or until firm.

fruit salad

Chop up a combination of your favourite seasonal fruits to make an appealing "finger food" for your child. Serve with custard or yogurt, if desired.

☺TIP Choose seedless grapes, or halve seeded grapes and remove seeds for toddlers under the age of four.

frozen yogurt yum! yum!

snacking and finger food

QUICK SALMON PATE

These recipes are designed to add variety to the range of foods your toddler is now eating. Although we call them snacks, any of them could form the basis of a meal, and all of them pass the ultimate toddler test: they can be picked up and eaten with the fingers! They are ideal for that time of the afternoon when lunch seems a long time ago, dinner is still some way off and food of some sort is definitely called for – after all, just *being* 2 or 3 years old uses the most amazing amount of energy! A nutritious snack is also useful if your toddler is the "grazing" variety, who wants small amounts of food fairly frequently.

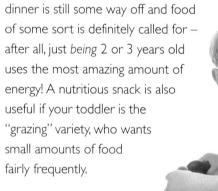

quick salmon pate

This is a versatile recipe: you can serve it on toast at breakfast, as a sandwich filling at lunch, or tossed through hot pasta for dinner.

105g can red salmon, drained
60g packaged cream cheese
1/4 cup (60ml) mayonnaise
2 teaspoons lemon juice
2 teaspoons chopped fresh parsley
40g butter, softened
6 slices multi-grain bread

Remove skin and bones from salmon; process salmon, cheese, mayonnaise, juice, parsley and butter until pureed. Remove crusts from bread; using a rolling pin, flatten bread. Cut each bread slice into 4 triangles; place on oven tray.

Toast under grill or in a moderate oven about 15 minutes or until crisp and browned lightly; cool on wire rack. Serve pate with toast triangles.

MAKES 1 CUP PATE

Storage Pate, covered, in refrigerator up to 2 days; Toasts, airtight container up to 1 week

popcorn

1 tablespoon vegetable oil
¼ cup (55g) popping corn

Heat oil in large pan; cook popcorn,
covered tightly, over medium heat, shaking
occasionally, until popping
stops. Remove pan from heat; cool before
serving.

MAKES ABOUT 5 CUPS

Storage Airtight container, up to 2 days

☺TIP Popcorn can also be prepared
in a microwave oven. Place corn,
without oil, in microwave-safe jug;
cover tightly with plastic wrap,
cook on HIGH (100%) about
3 minutes or until
popping stops.

**Do not serve to
|toddlers under
3 years of age**

French onion dip

⅔ cup (160ml) sour cream
**1 tablespoon French onion
soup mix**

Combine ingredients in small bowl; serve
with toddler's favourite raw or blanched
vegetables.

MAKES ⅔ CUP

Storage Covered,
in refrigerator,
up to 2 days

FRENCH ONION DIP
WITH VEGETABLES

SAUSAGE ROLLS

simple sausage rolls

**1 sheet ready-rolled
puff pastry**
2 teaspoons milk
**4 (240g) thin beef
sausages**
**2 teaspoons stale
breadcrumbs**

Cut pastry sheet in half;
brush with half the milk. Place
2 sausages, end to end, along
centre of each pastry half; trim
sausages to fit pastry. Roll pastry
to enclose sausages; place, seam-
side down, on oiled oven tray.

Brush with remaining milk,
sprinkle with breadcrumbs. Bake
in moderately hot oven about
15 minutes or until pastry is
browned lightly and sausages are
cooked through. Cut each roll
diagonally into 5 pieces. Serve
with tomato sauce, if desired.

MAKES 10

Storage Covered, in refrigerator, up
to 2 days
Freeze Uncooked sausage
rolls suitable

POPCORN

basic scones

2¹/₂ cups (375g) self-raising flour
1 tablespoon caster sugar
¹/₄ teaspoon salt
30g butter
³/₄ cup (180ml) milk
¹/₂ cup (125ml) water,
approximately

Grease 23cm square slab cake pan. Place flour, sugar and salt in medium bowl; rub in butter with fingertips. Using a knife, stir in milk and enough water to make a soft, sticky dough.

Turn dough onto floured surface; knead quickly and lightly until smooth. Use hand to press dough out evenly to 2cm thickness; cut into 5cm rounds.

Gently knead scraps of dough together; repeat pressing and cutting out of dough. Place scones in prepared pan; bake in very hot oven about 15 minutes or until scones are browned and sound hollow when tapped. Turn onto wire rack to cool. Serve with jam and cream, if desired.

MAKES 16

Freeze Cooked or uncooked scones suitable

☺ TIP If you prefer crusty scones, cool uncovered. To soften crust, wrap hot scones in a tea-towel.

cheesy pumpkin and zucchini scones

2¹/₂ cups (375g) self-raising flour
1 tablespoon caster sugar
¹/₄ teaspoon salt
30g butter
¹/₄ cup (50g) finely
grated pumpkin
¹/₄ cup (50g) finely
grated zucchini
¹/₄ cup (30g) finely grated
cheddar cheese
³/₄ cup (180ml) milk
¹/₄ cup (60ml) water,
approximately
2 tablespoons finely grated
parmesan cheese

Grease 23cm square slab cake pan. Place flour, sugar and salt into large bowl; rub in butter with fingertips. Stir in pumpkin, zucchini and cheddar cheese. Using a knife, stir in milk and enough water to make a soft, sticky dough.

Proceed as in Basic Scone recipe above. Before baking scones, sprinkle with parmesan cheese.

MAKES 16

FROM BACK: CHEESY PUMPKIN AND ZUCCHINI SCONES AND APRICOT WHOLEMEAL SCONES

apricot wholemeal scones

¹/₂ cup (75g) finely chopped
dried apricots
¹/₂ cup (125ml) boiling water
1¹/₂ cups (225g) self-raising flour
1 cup (160g) wholemeal
self-raising flour
1 tablespoon caster sugar
¹/₄ teaspoon salt
30g butter
³/₄ cup (180ml) milk,
approximately

Grease 23cm square slab cake pan. Place apricots in small heatproof bowl, add the boiling water; stand 15 minutes. Place flours, sugar and salt in large bowl; rub in butter with fingertips. Using a knife, stir in undrained apricot mixture and enough milk to make a soft, sticky dough.

Proceed as in Basic Scone recipe above.

MAKES 16

chicken corn pouches

150g minced chicken
2 tablespoons corn kernels
2 teaspoons light soy sauce
1 green onion, chopped finely
pinch five-spice powder
**2 tablespoons canned finely
    chopped water chestnuts**
16 x 12.5cm spring roll wrappers
1 egg, beaten lightly
vegetable oil, for deep frying

Combine chicken, corn, sauce, onion, spice and chestnuts in small bowl; mix well. Place rounded teaspoon of chicken mixture on centre of each wrapper; brush around edge with egg, form into pouch shape, pinch to seal.

Deep-fry pouches in hot oil, in batches, until browned and cooked through. Drain on absorbent paper.
Serve with plum sauce, if desired.

MAKES 16

Best prepared on day of use; deep-fry just before serving

Freeze Uncooked pouches suitable

CHICKEN CORN POUCHES

vegetable pakoras

50g cauliflower florets
50g broccoli florets
1/4 cup (35g) plain flour
1 tablespoon cornflour
1 tablespoon polenta
1/2 teaspoon chicken salt
1 egg white
1/4 cup (60ml) water
**1/2 small (45g) zucchini,
    sliced thickly**
**1/2 small (125g) kumara,
    sliced thickly**
vegetable oil, for deep-frying

Boil, steam or microwave cauliflower and broccoli, separately, until just tender; drain. Place flours, polenta and salt in small bowl; stir in egg white and water, mix to smooth batter. Dip vegetables in batter to coat completely. Deep-fry vegetables in hot oil, in batches, until browned lightly and crisp. Drain on absorbent paper.

MAKES 2 SERVINGS

Best made just before serving

☺TIP Pappadums can be healthy snacks: simply cook, 1 at a time, in the microwave oven on HIGH (100%) about 50 seconds or until puffed and crisp. Serve alone or with dips to toddlers over 3 years of age.

VEGETABLE PAKORAS

TOMATO SAVOURIES

RICE-PAPER VEGIE ROLLS

tomato savouries

Oyster cases or small vol au vents are round or oval pastry cases made of puff or flaky pastry. They are available in supermarkets in packages of 12.

12 oyster cases
1 button mushroom, chopped finely
1/3 cup (80ml) bottled tomato pasta sauce

Place oyster cases on oven tray; bake in moderate oven 5 minutes.

Meanwhile, combine mushroom and sauce in small pan; cook, stirring, until hot. Fill cases just before serving; refrigerate or freeze remaining sauce for use in other snacks.

MAKES 12

Storage Sauce, covered, in refrigerator up to 4 days
Oyster cases, in airtight container, up to 1 week
Freeze Sauce and oyster cases suitable

rice-paper vegie rolls

We used bean thread vermicelli for this simple recipe which makes a healthy snack for children and adults alike.

25g bean thread vermicelli
2 teaspoons smooth peanut butter
2 teaspoons hot water

4 sheets rice paper
1/4 small (50g) avocado, sliced thinly
1/2 small (35g) carrot, grated finely
2 tablespoons finely grated fresh beetroot
1 green onion, sliced finely

DIPPING SAUCE

2 tablespoons sugar
2 tablespoons water
1 tablespoon white vinegar
1/2 (65g) Lebanese cucumber, seeded, chopped finely

Place vermicelli in small heatproof bowl, cover with boiling water, stand only until just tender; drain. Cut noodles into 4cm lengths; combine in small bowl with peanut butter and the hot water. Place 1 sheet of rice paper in medium bowl of warm water until just softened; lift out carefully, place on board. Place layer of noodle mixture in centre of rice paper; top with avocado, carrot, beetroot and onion. Roll to enclose, folding in ends.

Repeat with remaining rice paper sheets and filling ingredients. Serve with Dipping Sauce.

Dipping Sauce Combine sugar and water in small pan; stir over low heat, without boiling, until sugar dissolves. Simmer, uncovered, 2 minutes; stir in vinegar, cool. Stir in cucumber.

MAKES 4

Best assembled just before serving

MUSHROOMS, PEAS, HAM AND
CREAM NOODLES

using your noodle

Most small children adore instant noodles and from the cook's point of view they're a good idea as well, since they're ready in minutes, provide a satisfying serve of energy-giving carbohydrates, and can be combined with an infinite variety of ingredients to suit the taste and appetite of even the fussiest eater. Instant noodles can be purchased in a plain, unflavoured form, but if you're using the sort that come with a flavour sachet, be aware that this flavouring can taste very strong to a young palate and is often rather too salty. When preparing the noodles for a child, either discard the flavour sachet altogether, or only use a very small amount, then combine the noodles with the ingredients of your choice, or try one of the suggestions listed here:

• tuna, green onions and tomato • mushrooms, peas, ham and a little cream
• chicken with creamed corn or corn kernels • stir-fried mixed vegetables

corn and capsicum pikelets

1 cup (150g) self-raising flour
³/4 cup (180ml) milk
1 egg
20g butter, melted
130g can creamed corn
2 green onions, chopped finely
**¹/4 cup (40g) finely chopped
red capsicum**
**¹/4 cup (30g) coarsely grated
cheddar cheese**

Place flour in medium bowl; gradually stir in combined milk, egg and butter; mix to a smooth batter. Stir in remaining ingredients. Drop ¹/4 cups of mixture, in batches, into heated oiled heavy-base pan, cook until bubbles appear; turn pikelets, cook until brown. Serve with sour cream.

MAKES 8

Storage Covered, in refrigerator, up to 2 days
Freeze Suitable

potato and onion pikelets

1 cup (150g) self-raising flour
³/4 cup (180ml) milk
1 egg
20g butter, melted
1 clove garlic, crushed
**1 small (80g) onion,
grated coarsely**
**1 small (120g) potato,
grated coarsely**

Place flour in medium bowl; gradually stir in combined milk, egg and butter; mix to a smooth batter. Stir in remaining ingredients. Drop ¹/4 cups of mixture, in batches, into heated oiled heavy-base pan, cook until bubbles appear; turn pikelets, cook until brown. Serve with sour cream.

MAKES 8

Storage Covered, in refrigerator, up to 2 days
Freeze Suitable

BROWNIES

brownies

150g butter
**1 cup (200g) firmly packed
brown sugar**
2 eggs
¹/2 cup (75g) plain flour
¹/2 cup (50g) cocoa
**¹/2 cup (60g) finely
chopped pecans**

Grease deep 19cm square cake pan, line base and sides with baking paper. Beat butter and sugar in small bowl with electric mixer until light and fluffy. Add eggs, 1 at a time, beating until just combined between additions. Stir in sifted flour and cocoa then nuts; spread mixture into prepared pan. Bake in slow oven about 30 minutes; cool in pan. Cut into small squares; dust with sifted icing sugar, if desired.

Storage Airtight container, up to 4 days
Freeze Suitable

Delete nuts if serving to toddlers under 5 years of age

FROM BACK: POTATO AND ONION PIKELETS AND CORN AND CAPSICUM PIKELETS

THE VANILLA BEINGS

the vanilla beings

Cutters of many shapes and sizes are available from kitchen shops and department stores. The number of shapes you get from one quantity of dough will depend on the size of cutters you use: we used a 9cm gingerbread cutter here. You also need assorted food colourings, piping bags and lollies to decorate these biscuits.

125g butter
1 teaspoon vanilla essence
2/3 cup (150g) caster sugar
2 eggs, beaten lightly
2 teaspoons milk
1 1/3 cups (200g) self-raising flour
1 cup (150g) plain flour

ICING
2 egg whites
3 1/2 cups icing sugar mixture

Beat butter, essence and sugar in medium bowl with electric mixer until smooth.

Add eggs, one at a time; beat until just combined. Stir in milk and flours; mix to a soft dough. Knead dough on floured surface until smooth, cover; refrigerate 30 minutes. Roll dough between sheets of baking paper until 5mm thick. Using 9cm cutter; cut shapes from dough, re-rolling dough as necessary.

Place shapes, about 3cm apart, on lightly greased oven trays; bake in moderate oven about 10 minutes or until biscuits are firm and browned lightly. Stand 5 minutes; lift biscuits onto wire racks to cool.

Icing Beat egg whites in medium bowl with electric mixer until soft peaks form; gradually beat in icing sugar. Divide among as many small bowls as you need for different colours; tint as desired with food colourings.

Spoon icing into piping bags fitted with small plain tubes; decorate cold biscuits as desired with icing and lollies.

MAKES ABOUT 20

Storage Airtight container, up to 1 week
Freeze Un-iced biscuits suitable

ice blocks

For variety, try using other fruit juice flavours, cordial or soft drink.

¹/₂ cup (125ml) natural yogurt
2 cups (500ml) apple juice
1 cup (250ml) blackcurrant juice

Place yogurt in large jug, gradually whisk in apple juice. Pour half the yogurt mixture into twelve ¹/₃-cup (80ml-capacity) ice block moulds or paper cups; freeze until almost set. Insert a pop stick into centre of ice-block; return to freezer until set. Pour blackcurrant juice on top of frozen yogurt layer; freeze until firm. Top with remaining yogurt mixture; freeze until firm.

MAKES 12

☺TIP Vary the flavour and texture of these ice blocks by using juice or syrup from canned fruit, diluted to taste.

ICE BLOCKS

QUICK APPLE TARTS

goody bags

Prepare a bag of mixed treats – they are ideal for a snack pack to carry in your backpack and for your child when he's travelling in the stroller. Create your own selection or try one of the suggestions listed here:

- fruit sticks • apricot and coconut slice
- pretzels • small savoury biscuit shapes
- small sweet biscuits • sultanas

smoothie

We used fresh strawberries here but a banana or 1/2 cup of rockmelon pieces also make a great smoothie.

1/2 cup (125ml) milk
1/2 cup sliced strawberries
1/4 cup (60ml) strawberry yogurt

Blend all ingredients until smooth.
MAKES ABOUT 1 CUP (250ml)
Best made just before serving

quick apple tarts

1 sheet ready-rolled puff pastry
40g butter, melted
1 medium (150g) apple, cored, sliced thinly
1 tablespoon brown sugar
1 tablespoon caster sugar
1 tablespoon icing sugar mixture

Cut pastry into 9 squares; place on greased oven tray. Using half the butter, brush each square; divide apple slices among squares, brush with remaining butter. Sprinkle with combined brown and caster sugars; bake in hot oven about 30 minutes or until puffed and browned lightly. Lift onto wire rack to cool; dust with icing sugar before serving.
MAKES 9

Storage Covered, in refrigerator, up to 2 days
Freeze Uncooked tarts suitable

SMOOTHIE

portable food and lunchboxes

Aside from occasionally being a necessity, portable food is another excellent way of making a mealtime enjoyable for your toddler. Even if you only sit on a rug at the end of your garden, the idea of a picnic almost invariably appeals to a small child and presents a wonderful opportunity for involving her in the preparations and sense of adventure. For the difficult eater, too, taking a meal into different surroundings can defuse a stressful situation and, with any luck, create renewed interest in eating. And if it does neither of those things, at least you can enjoy the sunshine and rejoice that this is one meal you won't need to scrape from the walls!

Eating outdoors

Whether you're in the garden or in the local park with the neighbourhood mums, you should choose food that is easy to pack and carry and, of course, easy to eat with the fingers. It's a good idea to invest in an inexpensive set of plastic boxes of varying sizes, all with tight-fitting lids, as well as some unbreakable beakers or plastic screw-top bottles, for drinks. And don't forget washcloths or tissues – the potential for mess remains fairly constant!

Eating and travel

When considering a journey with small children, it is sensible to take along a cool bag or small cooler box, as food can deteriorate quickly in a hot car. Pack lots of small snack-type foods and plenty of fluids – children become irritable when constrained for any length of time and snacking is a sure way to divert their attention and keep up flagging energy levels. You should take care, however, when travelling alone with small toddlers, to give them only food that they cannot choke on – if you are in any doubt, stop the car so that you can supervise the snack.

The lunchbox

A plastic lunchbox is an ideal way of presenting food to a curious toddler, as well as being useful to transport a meal when the need arises.

Most pre-schools serve their own meals these days, so you will probably not need to pack lunch with the monotonous regularity that happens once school starts. But there are still sure to be lots of times when a packed lunchbox will come in handy, as well as providing fun and variety in your toddler's meals. Older pre-schoolers also love the idea of having their own "grown up" lunchbox, ready for school.

Some lunchboxes come with a fitted plastic drink bottle that doubles as a food cooler when filled with cold or frozen drink. This is ideal because it enables you to provide water or to dilute juice as you wish, but a cold tetra-pack is a convenient, if more expensive, alternative.

MINI-GRISSINI, VEGETABLE STICKS AND DIP

Tempting children to lunch

• When packing a lunchbox, consider the age of the child as well as how long you need the food to keep before it is consumed – even the most valiant of eaters will probably suffer a loss of appetite when faced with The Soggy Tomato Sandwich.

• Pre-schoolers are far more likely to be tempted by lots of small packages of different things than one big sandwich and a piece of fruit. In fact, it's a rare toddler indeed who will eat a whole piece of fruit, so cut it into smaller portions, wrapping them individually to prevent browning – or try mini-containers of grapes or melon cubes.

• Dried fruit is an alternative to soggy or wasted fresh fruit and there is a wide variety available both from supermarkets and health food stores.

• Cut sandwiches into interesting shapes using a cookie cutter.

• As a change from your usual loaf, roll grated salad ingredients into lavash bread and cut into mini-rolls.

• Create a triple-decker effect, using brown and white bread alternately with simple fillings, such as ham, cream cheese and lettuce. Slice sandwich into fingers and pack on their sides so that the child can see the layers.

• Make sliced bread into "rolls" by removing crusts and flattening slightly. Spread with a simple filling, such as Vegemite, Marmite, peanut butter or ham, and roll up. Wrap tightly in plastic wrap, refrigerate, then slice into rounds about 1cm thick when cold.

• Instead of serving a salad sandwich, cut favourite foods, such as bread, tomato, cheese, ham and celery, into bite-size bits and serve in a small lettuce-leaf cup as a finger-food salad.

• Mix chopped leftover cooked potatoes with mayonnaise. Spoon into a lettuce leaf with cold cooked chicken or chopped hard-boiled egg, tomato and other salad ingredients.

• Cold cooked rice tossed with a little French dressing and chopped celery, capsicum, sultanas, orange segments and chopped cooked chicken makes a delicious change.

• Make interesting salads from cold noodles or pasta – just add bite-size bits of the foods you know your toddler enjoys.

• Serve cubes of mild cheese with a small bowl of chopped fruit.

• Serve crackers or mini-grissini with dips for a change from bread.

popular toddler lunch boxes

MINI LAVASH ROLLS

RICE SALAD

CHEESE, ROCKMELON
AND GRAPES

Food to go

Wherever you're travelling, carrying prepared snacks will save you having to resort to expensive and nutritionally dubious fast food.

HUMMUS

SAVOURY MUFFINS

TURKEY AND CHEESE ROLLUPS

savoury muffins

2 cups (300g) self-raising flour
1/2 cup (60g) finely chopped ham
1/2 cup (60g) coarsely grated cheddar cheese
1/4 cup (20g) finely chopped mushrooms
1 small (150g) red capsicum, chopped finely
1 tablespoon finely chopped fresh parsley
125g butter, melted
1 cup (250ml) milk
1 egg, beaten lightly

Grease three 12-hole small (2-tablespoon/40ml-capacity) muffin pans.

Combine flour, ham, cheese, mushrooms, capsicum and parsley in large bowl. Stir in butter, milk and egg; do not overmix. Divide mixture among pan holes. Bake in moderately hot oven 15 minutes; turn onto wire rack to cool.

MAKES 30

Storage Covered, in refrigerator, up to 2 days
Freeze Suitable

turkey and cream cheese roll-ups

1 piece lavash
1 tablespoon spreadable cream cheese
3 slices (65g) smoked turkey
3 cheese slices
3 iceberg lettuce leaves
1 small (60g) egg tomato, sliced thinly

Spread bread with cream cheese. Place turkey, cheese, lettuce and tomato on lavash; roll tightly then cut into quarters.

MAKES 4 SERVINGS

Best made on day of serving

hummus

2 teaspoons lemon juice
1 clove garlic
1/2 teaspoon ground cumin
3/4 cup (130g) drained canned chickpeas
1/4 cup (60ml) milk
1 teaspoon tahini
2 teaspoons finely chopped fresh coriander leaves

Blend or process all ingredients until smooth. Serve with mini-grissini.

MAKES 1 1/2 CUPS (375ml)

Storage Covered, in refrigerator, up to 2 days

toddler ploughman's lunch

We used French-onion dip in this recipe, but try other varieties such as salmon or avocado.

¹/₂ small (70g) carrot
3 asparagus spears, trimmed
3 snow peas, trimmed
I slice (40g) corned beef
50g cheddar cheese, cubed
I small (60g) egg tomato, quartered
2 tablespoons packaged French-onion dip
I bread roll

Cut carrot into sticks. Boil, steam or microwave carrot, asparagus and snow peas, separately, until just tender; drain.
Arrange all ingredients in lunchbox or on plate.

MAKES I SERVING

Best made just before serving

SALMON RICE LOAF

muesli bar

We suggest that only toddlers aged over three be given this as a treat.

125g butter
¹/₂ cup (100g) firmly packed brown sugar
I tablespoon honey
2 cups (180g) rolled oats
¹/₄ cup (35g) sesame seeds, toasted
¹/₄ cup (40g) sunflower seeds, chopped finely
¹/₄ cup (20g) desiccated coconut, toasted
¹/₄ cup (30g) finely chopped pecans or walnuts
¹/₄ cup (40g) sultanas
2 tablespoons unprocessed bran
¹/₂ teaspoon ground cinnamon

Grease 20cm x 30cm lamington pan. Combine butter, sugar and honey in medium pan; stir over low heat until sugar dissolves. Stir in remaining ingredients. Press mixture into prepared pan; bake in moderate oven about 25 minutes or until browned lightly. While still warm, cut through bar into 15 pieces; cool in pan.

MAKES 15

Storage Airtight container, up to 4 days

salmon rice loaf

You will need a little over ¹/₃ cup uncooked calrose rice for this recipe.

415g can red salmon, drained, flaked
I cup cooked calrose rice
I cup (70g) stale breadcrumbs
I cup (250ml) sour cream
I small (80g) onion, chopped finely
3 eggs, beaten lightly
I tablespoon finely chopped fresh parsley
I teaspoon French mustard
I teaspoon finely grated lemon rind
2 tablespoons lemon juice

Oil 15cm x 25cm loaf pan, line base with baking paper. Combine all ingredients in large bowl; mix well. Spoon mixture into prepared pan, smooth top; bake in moderately hot oven about I hour or until set. Stand 10 minutes; turn onto wire rack.

MAKES 8 SERVINGS

Storage Covered, in refrigerator, up to 2 days

TODDLER PLOUGHMAN'S LUNCH

MUESLI BAR

Pint-sized picnic fare

They might be devised for toddlers but adults will also enjoy these delicious and easily transported picnic foods – just make enough for the whole family.

Mediterranean meatballs

If fresh herbs are not available, use ¹/2 teaspoon each dried mint and basil.

MEDITERRANEAN MEATBALLS

500g minced beef
1 medium (120g) zucchini, grated coarsely
1 medium (120g) carrot, grated coarsely
1 small (80g) onion, chopped finely
¹/2 cup (35g) stale breadcrumbs
2 tablespoons tomato sauce
1 tablespoon finely chopped fresh mint leaves
1 tablespoon finely chopped fresh basil leaves
1 egg, beaten lightly

YOGURT CUCUMBER SAUCE
1 Lebanese (130g) cucumber, peeled, seeded
¹/2 cup (125ml) yogurt

Combine all meatball ingredients in medium bowl; using hands, roll tablespoons of mixture into balls.
Place on oiled oven tray; bake, uncovered, in moderate oven about 20 minutes or until cooked through.
Serve with Yogurt Cucumber Sauce.

Yogurt Cucumber Sauce Grate cucumber coarsely; place in strainer, allow to drain 20 minutes then combine with yogurt in small bowl.

MAKES 35

Storage Covered, in refrigerator, up to 2 days
Freeze Uncooked meatballs suitable

potato tortilla

This is a Spanish dish which is usually cut into wedges and eaten cold – so it's great for a picnic.

2 tablespoons olive oil
2 medium (400g) potatoes, sliced thinly
1 small (80g) onion, chopped finely
6 eggs, beaten lightly

Heat 1 tablespoon of the oil in 24cm non-stick pan; cook potatoes and onion, stirring, about 5 minutes or until potatoes are tender. Remove from pan; combine in medium bowl with eggs.
Heat remaining oil in same pan; pour in egg mixture. Cook, tilting pan, over medium heat until eggs are almost set. Place pan under heated grill until top is browned lightly. Serve hot or cold, cut into wedges.

MAKES 4 TO 8 SERVINGS

Storage Covered, in refrigerator, up to 2 days

sultana slice

125g butter
¹/2 cup (110g) caster sugar
2 eggs
¹/2 cup (75g) self-raising flour
¹/2 cup (75g) plain flour
1 ¹/2 cups (240g) sultanas

Grease 20cm x 30cm lamington pan, line base with baking paper. Beat butter and sugar in small bowl with electric mixer until light and fluffy. Add eggs, 1 at a time, beating well between additions. Stir in flours and sultanas; spread mixture into prepared pan. Bake in moderate oven about 25 minutes; cool in pan. Cut into fingers to serve.
Storage Airtight container, up to 4 days

submarine sandwich

Split a small French breadstick or long soft roll in half lengthwise; remove and discard some of the soft centre. Fill hollowed-out bread with whatever sandwich filling your children like best; slice and wrap in plastic until ready to eat.

PERFECT PICNICS

• Always travel with a rubber-backed picnic rug in your car, or a large sheet of plastic.

• Take a beach umbrella in case there is no shade.

• Toss in a thin tablecloth to throw over food to keep out the bugs.

• Don't forget hats, sunscreen and insect repellent.

• A sarong is the most versatile item to take on a picnic – it can double for almost anything, even as a carry-all for the baby.

• Freeze large containers of water – such as the clean bladder from a wine cask or a 2-litre fruit juice bottle – the night before. Large pieces of ice melt more slowly than crushed ice and, as it melts, you'll have fresh, cold drinking water.

• Pack perishables in a cooler box or insulated bag and non-perishables in a basket.

• A wide-mouth vacuum flask is a great investment for winter picnics – all kinds of food can be kept hot, including food for small babies.

• Take a rubbish bag and a bag for dirty plates, beakers and containers.

• Take damp facecloths in a plastic container for wiping dirty hands and faces.

• Don't forget that a long outing may include morning and afternoon tea as well as lunch – make sure you have enough supplies for the whole day.

CLOCKWISE FROM LEFT:
SUBMARINE SANDWICH;
SULTANA SLICE;
POTATO TORTILLA

crispy drumettes

12 large (1.5kg) chicken wings
1/4 cup (35g) plain flour
1 egg, beaten lightly
1/4 cup (60ml) milk
**3/4 cup (80g) finely crushed
    corn chips**
1 tablespoon olive oil

Remove and discard tip from each wing; cut wings in half at joint. Using meaty half of wing (freeze remaining half), hold small end of each piece, trim around bone to cut meat free; cut, scrape and push meat towards large end. Pull skin and meat down over end of bone; each wing piece will resemble a baby drumstick.

Toss wings in flour, shake away excess; dip in combined egg and milk then in corn chips. Place wings on greased oven tray; drizzle with oil. Bake, uncovered, in moderate oven about 40 minutes or until wings are cooked and browned. Serve hot or cold.

MAKES 12

Storage Covered, in refrigerator, up to 2 days

cheese and spinach pie

Two 250g packages of frozen spinach, thawed and drained until all excess moisture is eliminated, can be substituted for fresh spinach.

1 tablespoon olive oil
**1 small (80g) onion,
    chopped finely**
3 green onions, chopped finely
1 clove garlic, crushed
500g spinach, trimmed, chopped
1 cup (200g) cottage cheese
**1/2 cup (100g) fetta
    cheese, crumbled**
**1/4 cup (20g) finely grated
    parmesan cheese**
**1/4 cup finely chopped
    fresh parsley**
4 eggs, beaten lightly
1/2 teaspoon mustard powder
1/4 teaspoon ground nutmeg
8 sheets fillo pastry
1/4 cup (60ml) olive oil, extra

CLOCKWISE FROM TOP LEFT: CHEESE AND SPINACH PIE; SALMON RICE LOAF (PAGE 61); CARROT AND PINEAPPLE CAKE; EASY SUMMER SALAD; AND CRISPY DRUMETTES

Grease 19cm × 29cm rectangular slice pan. Heat oil in large pan; cook onion and garlic, stirring, until onion is soft. Add spinach; cook, stirring, until just wilted. Transfer to large bowl; stir in cheeses, parsley, eggs, mustard and nutmeg.

To prevent pastry from drying out, cover with damp tea-towel until ready to use. Brush 1 sheet of pastry with oil, fold in half horizontally, ease into prepared pan; repeat with 3 more pastry sheets. Pour spinach mixture over pastry in pan; repeat brushing with oil, folding and placing remaining 4 sheets of pastry over spinach mixture, tucking edges down into side of pan. Brush top with oil; using sharp knife, mark uncooked pie into 8 portions. Bake in moderately hot oven about 30 minutes or until set.

SERVES 8

Storage Covered, in refrigerator, up to 2 days

easy summer salad

**6 small (720g) potatoes,
 chopped coarsely**
**2 medium (300g) apples, peeled,
 chopped coarsely**
¹/₂ cup (80g) sultanas
250g cherry tomatoes, halved
**¹/₄ cup (60ml) bottled
 coleslaw dressing**
¹/₄ cup (60ml) yogurt

Boil, steam or microwave potato until
tender; drain. Combine cooled potato
in large bowl with remaining ingredients;
toss gently.

SERVES 6 TO 8

Best made just before serving

carrot and pineapple cake

*You will need 2 medium (240g) carrots
for this cake.*

1³/₄ cups (260g) self-raising flour
¹/₂ teaspoon bicarbonate of soda
1 teaspoon ground cinnamon
³/₄ cup (165g) caster sugar
¹/₂ cup (60g) almond meal
²/₃ cup (60g) desiccated coconut
3 eggs, beaten lightly
¹/₂ cup (125ml) vegetable oil
³/₄ cup (180ml) yogurt
1¹/₂ cups coarsely grated carrot
**¹/₂ cup (130g) drained canned
 crushed pineapple**

Grease deep 19cm square cake pan,
line base with baking paper. Combine
combined flour, soda and cinnamon
in large bowl with sugar, almonds and
coconut. Stir in remaining ingredients.
Spread mixture into prepared pan; bake
in moderate oven 1 hour. Stand cake
10 minutes; turn onto wire rack to cool.
Just before serving, dust with icing sugar.

Storage Airtight container, in refrigerator, up
to 4 days
Freeze Suitable

sausage twist

500g sausage mince
1 cup (70g) stale breadcrumbs
2 green onions, chopped finely
2 tablespoons tomato sauce
2 teaspoons Worcestershire
   sauce
1 tablespoon fruit chutney
2 tablespoons finely chopped
   fresh parsley
1 clove garlic, crushed
1/2 teaspoon sweet paprika
1/2 teaspoon mixed spice
2 sheets ready-rolled
   shortcrust pastry
4 hard-boiled eggs, halved
1 tablespoon milk

Combine mince, breadcrumbs, onion, sauces, chutney, parsley, garlic and spices in large bowl. Place each sheet of pastry on a separate oiled and baking paper-lined oven tray. Spread a quarter of mince mixture along the centre of each pastry sheet; place 4 egg halves on top of each.

STEP 1
Using wet hand, gently press remaining mince mixture over egg halves.

STEP 2
Make diagonal cuts on pastry each side of the filling at 2cm intervals. Lift alternate strips of pastry over filling to resemble plait; tuck ends under; brush pastry plaits all over with milk. Bake in moderately hot oven about 35 minutes or until browned lightly; lift onto wire rack to cool.

MAKES 4 TO 6 SERVINGS

Storage Covered, in refrigerator, up to 2 days

SAUSAGE TWIST

mini suppli

Suppli is the Italian name of these delicious deep-fried balls of rice with their core of melted mozzarella.

10g butter
1 small (80g) onion, grated
1 clove garlic, crushed
1/3 cup (65g) calrose rice
2/3 cup (160ml) chicken stock
1 tablespoon tomato paste
2 tablespoons finely grated parmesan cheese
1 egg, beaten lightly
40g mozzarella cheese
1/4 cup (15g) stale breadcrumbs
vegetable oil, for deep-frying

Melt butter in small pan; cook onion and garlic, stirring, until onion is soft. Add rice; stir until coated with butter. Add combined stock and paste, bring to boil; simmer over low heat, covered, about 10 minutes or until rice is tender. Quickly stir parmesan and egg into rice; cool.

Cut mozzarella cheese in 12 even-size cubes. Using hand, mould 1 tablespoon of rice mixture around each mozzarella cube to make ball shape. Gently toss rice balls in breadcrumbs, cover; refrigerate about 2 hours or until firm.

Heat oil in large deep pan; deep-fry suppli, in batches, until browned lightly, drain on absorbent paper.

MAKES 12

Best made just before serving

MINI SUPPLI

salmon quichettes

1 sheet ready-rolled shortcrust pastry
1/2 cup (60g) grated cheddar cheese
105g can red salmon, drained, flaked
1/2 cup (125ml) milk
1 egg

Cut pastry into nine 7.5cm rounds; press pastry rounds into holes of greased shallow patty pan. Divide combined cheese and salmon among pastry cases.

Whisk together milk and egg in small jug; pour enough into each pastry case to cover filling. Bake in moderately hot oven about 20 minutes or until filling is set. Cool 5 minutes before removing quichettes from pan.

MAKES 9

Best made just before serving

SALMON QUICHETTES

scaloppine fingers

2 thin (175g) veal steaks
2 tablespoons plain flour
I egg, beaten lightly
**3/4 cup (75g) packaged
breadcrumbs**
vegetable oil, for shallow frying

Coat veal in flour, shake away excess; dip
into egg then coat in breadcrumbs. Place
in single layer on tray, cover; refrigerate
30 minutes. Shallow-fry veal in hot oil
until browned both sides and cooked
through. Serve sliced into fingers.

MAKES 4 SERVINGS

Best made just before serving

☺TIP Toddlers love to dip, so try
serving these crunchy veal fingers with
yogurt, or tomato, barbecue or sweet and
sour sauce.

BBQ CUTLETS

FROM BACK: BEANY LETTUCE
ROLL-UPS AND SCALOPPINE FINGERS

bbq cutlets

6 lamb cutlets
1/4 cup (60ml) barbecue sauce
1/4 cup (60ml) plum sauce

Trim cutlets of excess fat; brush each
cutlet with combined sauces. Cook
cutlets on heated oiled griddle (or grill
or barbecue) until browned both sides
and tender, brushing occasionally with
remaining combined sauces. Pack cooled
cutlets in lunch-box with salad and bread.

MAKES 6

Best made just before serving

Storage Covered, in refrigerator, up
to 2 days

beany lettuce roll-ups

*You will need 2/3 cup of uncooked
calrose rice for this recipe.*

2 cups cooked calrose rice
**300g can 4-bean mix,
drained, rinsed**
**I small (130g) apple, peeled,
chopped finely**
I celery stick, chopped finely
I green onion, chopped finely
1/4 cup (40g) sultanas
1/4 cup (60ml) French dressing
6 large cos lettuce leaves

Combine rice, beans, apple, celery, onion,
sultanas and dressing in a large bowl.
Divide filling mixture among lettuce
leaves; roll securely to form parcels.

MAKES 6

Best rolled just before serving

Storage Filling, covered, in refrigerator up
to 2 days

nachos to go

175g small savoury biscuits
200g prepared avocado dip
**1/2 cup (100g) canned kidney
beans, drained**
**I small (130g) tomato,
chopped finely**
**1/2 cup (60g) coarsely grated
cheddar cheese**

Arrange biscuits on serving plate.
Spoon dip and combined
beans and tomato over the
top; sprinkle with cheese,
serve immediately.

MAKES 6 SERVINGS

☺TIP You can
use any small
savoury biscuit,
rusks, mini-Ritz or
even cornchips if
your toddler is old
enough to chew
properly.

NACHOS TO GO

vegetable and cheese tarts

1 sheet ready-rolled shortcrust pastry
¹/₂ small (65g) tomato, chopped finely
¹/₂ small (35g) carrot, chopped finely
¹/₂ small (45g) zucchini, chopped finely
¹/₄ cup (50g) drained canned kidney beans
2 tablespoons frozen peas, thawed
²/₃ cup (80g) finely grated cheddar cheese

Cut pastry into nine 7.5cm rounds; press pastry rounds into holes of oiled shallow patty pan, prick well with skewer or fork. Bake in moderately hot oven about 15 minutes or until browned lightly.

Meanwhile, combine tomato, carrot, zucchini, beans and peas in small bowl; divide mixture among pastry cases, sprinkle cheese over top of each. Bake tarts in moderate oven about 10 minutes or until cheese melts.

MAKES 9

Storage Covered in refrigerator, up to 1 day

chicken burritos

1¹/₄ cups (225g) coarsely chopped cooked chicken
¹/₄ cup (60ml) mayonnaise
¹/₄ cup (60ml) sour cream
3 x 20cm flour tortillas
1 cup (55g) finely shredded lettuce
2 small (260g) tomatoes, chopped finely
¹/₂ cup (60g) coarsely grated cheddar cheese

Combine chicken, mayonnaise and sour cream in medium bowl. Divide mixture, lettuce, tomato and cheese among tortillas; roll securely to enclose filling. Cut in half to serve.

MAKES 6

Best made just before serving

RIGHT FROM TOP: VEGETABLE AND CHEESE TARTS; CHICKEN BURRITOS

Fruit, the all-time favourite

Chopped and fresh or incorporated into muffins and cakes, fruit is versatile, nutritious and always popular.

little pear and cinnamon cakes

1 medium (230g) pear
1/2 cup (125ml) vegetable oil
1/3 cup (75g) caster sugar
1 egg
1/2 cup (75g) plain flour
1/2 cup (75g) self-raising flour
1/4 teaspoon ground cinnamon
1/2 teaspoon caster sugar, extra

Grease two small 12-hole (2-tablespoon/40ml-capacity) muffin pans. Peel and halve pear, remove and discard core; chop into 1cm pieces. Whisk oil, sugar and egg together in medium bowl.

Add flours and pear; stir until just combined. Drop level tablespoons of mixture into each pan hole; sprinkle with combined cinnamon and extra caster sugar. Bake in moderately hot oven about 15 minutes. Turn onto wire rack; serve warm or cold.

MAKES 24

Storage Airtight container, up to 3 days

FRUIT CRUMBLE

LITTLE PEAR AND CINNAMON CAKES

fruit crumble

1 small (180g) pear
1 small (130g) apple
2 teaspoons caster sugar
1/2 cup (80g) wholemeal plain flour
60g butter, chopped coarsely
**1/4 cup (50g) tightly packed
   brown sugar**
1 tablespoon rolled oats
mixed spice

Peel, core and thinly slice pear and apple; place in greased shallow 2-cup (500ml) capacity ovenproof dish, sprinkle caster sugar over the top. Place flour in small bowl, rub in butter until mixture resembles breadcrumbs; stir in brown sugar and oats. Sprinkle over fruit, dust with mixed spice. Bake in moderate oven about 25 minutes or until just browned.

MAKES
2 SERVINGS

Storage Covered, in refrigerator, up to 2 days

fruit fantastic

Don't just chop it and serve it — with a little extra thought, fruit will tempt even the fussiest eater — and with so much to choose from, something is sure to appeal.

Nashi pear makes a sweet and crunchy alternative to more commonplace pears. Yummy with cheese cubes!

As an occasional special treat, dip ripe strawberries in melted chocolate — milk, dark or white.

Frozen peeled segments of orange and mandarin make marvellous thirst quenchers on a hot day.

Easy to digest, sweet rockmelon (and its cousin, the pretty green honeydew) can be served simply in fingers or chunks.

A perfect snack pack, kiwi fruit can be scooped from the skin with a spoon.

Always popular, grapes should be seeded and peeled for tiny tots.

A change from plain apple is to dip peeled quarters into a mixture of sugar and a little cinnamon.

Watermelon is always a favourite. For littlies, try to remove as many seeds as possible.

Score the flesh of mango cheeks into bite-size chunks, as shown, then press skin gently upwards for an easy-to-eat tropical treat.

Serve banana chunks with sweet, fresh dates (remove seeds), or insert a pop stick and make Monkey Tails (see recipe on page 104)

rock cakes

2 cups (300g) self-raising flour
1/4 teaspoon ground cinnamon
90g butter, chopped coarsely
1/3 cup (75g) caster sugar
1 cup (160g) sultanas
1/2 cup (125ml) milk,
approximately
1 egg, beaten lightly
1 tablespoon caster sugar, extra

Sift flour and cinnamon into large bowl;
rub in butter, stir in sugar and sultanas.
Stir in egg, then enough milk to mix to
a moist but firm dough; drop heaped
tablespoons of mixture 5cm apart onto
greased oven trays. Sprinkle a little extra
caster sugar over top of each cake; bake
in moderately hot oven about 15 minutes
or until browned lightly. Loosen cakes;
cool on trays.

MAKES 18

Storage Airtight container, up to 3 days

apricot bars

If there are any large pieces of nuts in the
muesli, chop finely to avoid the risk of choking.

185g butter
2 tablespoons golden syrup
1/4 cup (35g) self-raising flour
1/4 cup (35g) plain flour
1/2 cup (55g) natural muesli
1/2 cup (100g) brown sugar
1/2 cup (75g) finely chopped
dried apricots
1/4 cup (40g) sultanas
1/4 cup (20g) rolled oats
1/4 cup (20g) desiccated coconut
2 eggs, beaten lightly

Grease 20cm x 30cm lamington pan; line
base with baking paper.
   Combine butter and syrup in small
pan; stir over low heat until butter melts.
Combine sifted flours, muesli, sugar,
apricots, sultanas, oats and coconut
together in large bowl; stir in eggs and
cooled butter mixture.
   Press mixture into prepared pan; bake
in moderate oven 25 minutes. Cool in
pan; cut into fingers before serving.

Storage Airtight container, up to 4 days

ROCK CAKES

APRICOT BARS

chunky chocolate cookies

I egg
¹/₂ cup (100g) firmly packed brown sugar
¹/₄ cup (60ml) vegetable oil
²/₃ cup (100g) plain flour
¹/₂ cup (75g) self-raising flour
¹/₄ teaspoon bicarbonate of soda
100g dark chocolate, melted
³/₄ cup (110g) dark chocolate Melts

CHOCOLATE ICING
20g butter, melted
75g dark chocolate, melted
²/₃ cup (110g) icing sugar mixture
2 teaspoons milk, approximately

Beat egg and sugar in medium bowl with electric mixer about
1 minute or until mixture changes colour. Stir in oil and sifted dry
ingredients then cooled melted chocolate (mixture will be soft).
Cover, refrigerate 1 hour.

Roll heaped teaspoons of mixture into balls; place 5cm
apart on greased oven trays. Bake in moderately hot oven
about 8 minutes or until cracked and slightly firm. Stand on trays
5 minutes before turning onto wire racks to cool.

Spread top of each cookie with Chocolate Icing and top with
dark chocolate Melts. Dust with icing sugar mixture, if desired.

Chocolate Icing Combine cooled butter and chocolate with
sifted icing sugar mixture in small bowl. Stir in enough milk to
make a soft paste.

MAKES ABOUT 3 DOZEN

Storage Airtight container, up to 4 days

CHUNKY CHOCOLATE COOKIES

CRUNCHY COOKIES

crunchy cookies

90g butter
1/4 cup (60ml) honey
2 tablespoons golden syrup
1 cup (150g) self-raising flour
1 cup (90g) desiccated coconut
1 cup (30g) corn flakes
1/2 cup (160g) sultanas
1/2 cup (95g) dark Choc Bits

Combine butter, honey and golden syrup in medium pan; stir over heat until butter melts. Cool 5 minutes; stir in remaining ingredients, mix well. Drop level tablespoons of mixture about 5cm apart onto greased oven trays; bake in moderate oven about 12 minutes. Stand 5 minutes; turn onto wire racks to cool.

MAKES ABOUT 2 DOZEN

Storage Airtight container, up to 1 week

lemonade

1/2 cup (110g) sugar
1/2 cup (125ml) water
1/2 cup (125ml) lemon juice
3 cups (750ml) water, extra

Combine sugar and water in small pan; stir over low heat, without boiling, until sugar dissolves. Bring to boil; simmer, uncovered, 2 minutes. Stir in lemon juice, stand 30 minutes. Strain lemon mixture into large jug, add extra water; refrigerate until required.

MAKES 4 CUPS (1 LITRE)

fruit fizz

250g trimmed watermelon, chopped coarsely
250g trimmed pineapple, chopped coarsely
2 small (360g) oranges, peeled, chopped coarsely
1 cup (250ml) sparkling mineral water

Blend or process watermelon, pineapple and orange until smooth; strain juice into large jug. Just before serving, stir in mineral water.

MAKES 3 CUPS (750ml)

quick-mix banana cake

You need approximately 2 (460g) overripe bananas for this recipe.

125g butter
3/4 cup (150g) firmly packed brown sugar
2 eggs
1/3 cup (80ml) sour cream
1 1/2 cups (225g) self-raising flour
1/2 teaspoon bicarbonate of soda
1 cup mashed banana

LEMON ICING

1 cup (160g) icing sugar mixture
3 teaspoons soft butter
1 tablespoon lemon juice
2 teaspoons hot water, approximately

Grease deep 19cm square cake pan, line base with baking paper.

Beat butter and sugar in small bowl with electric mixer until light and fluffy. Add eggs, sour cream, flour and soda; beat on low speed 1 minute. Stir in banana; spread mixture into prepared pan. Bake in moderate oven 45 minutes. Stand cake 10 minutes; turn onto wire rack. When cold, top cake with Lemon Icing.

Lemon Icing Combine icing sugar, butter and juice in small bowl; stir in enough water to make a spreadable consistency.

Storage Airtight container, in refrigerator, up to 4 days

QUICK-MIX BANANA CAKE

drink it up, Poppy...

Although water is the best thirst quencher for busy tots, fruit drinks make a nourishing change and also provide a way of adding more fresh fruit to a toddler's diet.

FRUIT FIZZ (LEFT) AND
HOMEMADE LEMONADE

drink it...

adapting family meals

Delicate little purees are great when you're starting out, but there's no doubt that life gets a whole lot easier when your toddler starts eating the same meals as you – unless, of course, your family lives on greasy takeaway, in which case you might consider getting the rest of the family to eat what the toddler eats instead!

Adapting your family meals to suit the smallest member should really require very little extra effort. Obviously, you will need to cut things into bite-size pieces where appropriate, and for smaller toddlers you might still need to mash or grind some foods. But by and large, there is not much that a healthy toddler cannot eat, and most adaptation will be concerned with the texture or consistency rather than the ingredients. If your family meals involve curry, for instance, there is no reason why your toddler can't have curry too – simply reserve her portion before you add the chilli, then cut it up or puree as appropriate. This applies to all very strong tasting or salty foods – separate the child's portion before adding the "adult" ingredients, or add reduced amounts of strong spice to hers so she gets used to the taste gradually. Don't assume that everything she eats needs to be completely bland, however – it doesn't, and if you fall into this trap you might find yourself with a very unadventurous eater on your hands.

Of course, you might already have one of these on your hands and at low moments you'll have started to think you'll be serving mashed banana sandwiches at her wedding – if she's lucky enough to find a partner who shares her hatred of anything green! Don't despair. Keep serving the foods that you know she likes, but offer a little taste of what you're having as well – this is easier if she's actually at the table with you. Don't insist that it's eaten, and don't make an issue when it's not. Eventually, she will realise that it's not a power game and that some of the things she's tried from your plate are actually quite nice!

Adjusting your favourite recipes

Remember to stick with a commonsense approach and you'll find it easy to adapt family meals to healthy toddler food. You might even find your own diet becomes a little healthier as well!

• For a perfectly balanced diet that includes everything a growing body needs, try to include some of each of the 5 food groups in each meal (see page 81), but be realistic as well and keep your eye on the big picture – if your toddler eats a variety of food over the course of a week or so, one or two faddish meals are not going to result in malnutrition.

• When pureeing family food for younger babies, add a little boiled water, milk or salt-free stock to achieve the desired consistency.

• Consider the texture of what you are serving – tender meat is usually more attractive to a toddler, so bear this in mind when shopping.

• Reduce amounts of saturated fats, such as butter and cream, trim excess fat from meat and remove chicken skin. Remember, however,

that some fat is an essential part of the diet of babies and toddlers – dairy products should be full-fat unless your doctor advises otherwise.

• Use herbs, garlic and onion to add flavour to your cooking instead of relying on salt.

• Steaming or microwaving vegetables retains more nutrients. If boiling, use only small amounts of water and reserve the cooking liquid for stock. If peeling your vegies, do so very thinly as most nutrients are located just below the skin.

• Use non-stick pans to avoid the need for too much oil.

• Bake meat on a rack so that excess fat drips away.

• Even if your toddler is not actually eating at the table with you, remember to save a little of your meal and refrigerate or freeze for serving to him at a later time.

Opposite we give a sample weekly menu planner to show you how easy it is to choose meals that all the family will enjoy. Mix and match as you choose – but remember, you're not running a restaurant!

sample weekly menu planner

menu 1
MAIN   rice and vegetable soup
        chive and bacon
        damper
DESSERT   pear and ricotta strudel

menu 2
MAIN   baked potato, ham
        and cheese omelette
        mixed green salad
DESSERT   rhubarb and berry compote

menu 3
ENTREE   pumpkin and kumara soup
MAIN   rack of lamb with
        orange couscous
        mixed green salad

menu 4
ENTREE   rice paper vegie rolls
MAIN   glazed Thai chicken
        steamed jasmine rice
        mixed green salad

menu 5
MAIN   broadbean and leek pasta
        mixed green salad
DESSERT   baked orange cheesecake

menu 6
MAIN   Atlantic salmon with
        citrus butter sauce
DESSERT   quick-mix ice-cream
        and fruit salad

menu 7
MAIN   sunday roast
DESSERT   citrus delicious

Catering for vegetarians

Choosing vegetarianism for your baby can involve problems unless you go into it armed with adequate knowledge. To ensure your baby gets a well-balanced diet, the first thing you should do is seek advice from your doctor or early- childhood nurse.

A well-nourished vegetarian mother can provide all the nutrients her baby requires for the first 6 months of life through breast milk (or infant formula). Milk is vital in the first year of a child's life, so if you are choosing vegetarianism, it is a good idea to breastfeed as long as possible. Fortified formula can be used and soy-based infant formulas are also available. It is after it has been weaned and a child begins to eat family food that a strict vegetarian diet may cause problems.

If your vegetarian diet includes dairy products and eggs, it is fairly easy to provide all the nutritional requirements of a growing child. If fish can be added, providing adequate nourishment is even easier.

However, if you are a vegan (a diet of plant-based foods only), you may need to be a little more flexible when it comes to your baby's diet. This is because the strict regime of the vegan is really too bulky for a young child and may not include enough fat and protein for their many needs, particularly rapid growth.

When you are converting recipes to suit a vegetarian diet, don't simply remove the meat. Learn to combine two plant proteins (and increase the carbohydrate) so that the total mix of amino acids is sufficient to meet the child's needs. Meat substitutes can include pulses (such as baked beans), nutmeats, tofu or perhaps fish. Cheese or eggs can be added to many dishes for added protein and ground nuts – another source of protein – can be used to thicken sauces. Wherever possible, choose wholemeal pasta and breads and cook potatoes in their skin. Use milk, cheese, cottage cheese, yogurt and buttermilk as often as possible.

As with babies on a regular diet, introduce each new food one at a time and watch for an adverse reaction before starting the next new taste.

Principles of a balanced diet

Today's food is rather different to that eaten 30 or even 20 years ago – it is more varied and interesting and, quite often, lighter. However, the fundamental principles of good nutrition remain the same.

Planning balanced meals for your toddler is as easy as remembering to include a little of each of the Five Food Groups in daily meals to ensure that you are supplying all the essential nutrients needed for growth and good health.

Many toddlers are extremely fussy about what they will and won't eat; others have periods where they eat almost nothing at all and are unlikely to be impressed by your great knowledge of nutrition. Try to remain flexible and keep things in perspective – if you look at your toddler's diet over a week, rather than becoming obsessed with its shortcomings over a day, you will probably find that malnutrition is not as imminent as you thought!

And remember, too, that many different combinations of foods can supply all the necessary nutrients, so that your child's diet might vary considerably from a playmate's yet still be perfectly healthy. Don't forget the importance of water in any diet, and try to encourage your child to drink water from an early age. Fruit juice is a useful source of vitamin C, but a toddler does not need fruit juice every time she needs a drink – water is a far better thirst-quencher and will not cause tooth decay.

The five food groups

Breads, Grains and Cereals

This group provides carbohydrates for energy, as well as iron, B vitamins and fibre. Aim for six or more serves per day; one serve is 1 slice of bread or 2 to 3 crispbreads or 1/2 cup cooked pasta or rice.

Fruit, Vegetables and Salads

This group provides carbohydrates for energy, as well as iron and other minerals, calcium, several vitamins, including vitamin C, and fibre. Try for six or more serves per day; one serve is 1 piece of fruit or 1 medium potato or 1/2 cup vegetables or fruit salad or 150ml juice.

Milk and Dairy Products

This group provides calcium, protein, fat and several vitamins and minerals. Because babies require more fat than adults, the dairy products you serve to children should be full-fat unless medically advised. Three serves per day are recommended; one serve is 250ml milk or 200g yogurt or 30g cheese.

Fish, Meat and Eggs

This group is the major supply of protein, essential for growth and the repair of body cells. It is very easy to supply adequate protein to children on non-restrictive diets but vegetarians need to take care that enough protein is provided from non-meat sources, such as eggs, dairy products, soy beans and pulses. One serve per day is recommended; one serve is 150g fish or 125g meat/chicken or 2 eggs.

Fats and Oils

Although this is the food group you should eat least of, it is nonetheless an important source of vitamins A and D and should never be excluded entirely. For health's sake, the best fats are unsaturated (such as vegetable oils and nuts) rather than saturated (such as butter, cream or animal fat). One serve per day is recommended; one serve is 1 teaspoon oil or 1 tablespoon nuts (do not give whole nuts to children under 5 years).

rice and vegetable soup

1 tablespoon olive oil
**1 medium (150g) brown onion,
  chopped finely**
**1 trimmed (75g) celery stick,
  chopped finely**
**1 medium (120g) carrot,
  chopped coarsely**
1 litre (4 cups) vegetable stock
2 x 400g cans tomatoes
**420g can four-bean mix,
  rinsed, drained**
**1/2 cup (100g) long-grain
  white rice**
1/2 teaspoon sugar
**2 tablespoons finely chopped
  fresh basil leaves**
**1/3 cup (25g) finely grated
  parmesan cheese**

Heat oil in large pan; cook onion, celery
and carrot, stirring, until onion is soft.
Add stock, undrained crushed tomatoes,
beans, rice and sugar. Bring to boil; simmer,
uncovered, about 20 minutes
or until rice is tender. Serve soup
sprinkled with basil and cheese.

SERVES 4 TO 6

Storage Covered, in refrigerator,
up to 2 days
Freeze Suitable

☺ FOR BABY Puree to
the desired consistency

☺ FOR TODDLER
Chop to suit appropriate
stage of development

*RICE AND VEGETABLE SOUP,
SHOWN PUREED FOR BABY*

*RICE AND VEGETABLE SOUP,
TODDLER SERVE*

RICE AND VEGETABLE SOUP

chive and bacon damper

2 bacon rashers, chopped finely
2 cups (300g) self-raising flour
30g butter
**1/2 cup (60g) coarsely grated
  cheddar cheese**
**2 tablespoons finely chopped
  fresh chives**
1/2 cup (125ml) milk
**1/2 cup (125ml) water,
  aproximately**

Cook bacon in medium heated oiled pan,
stirring, until browned and crisp; drain on
absorbent paper.

Place flour in large bowl, rub in butter,
stir in cheese, chives and bacon. Add milk
and enough water to mix to a soft, sticky
dough. Turn dough onto floured surface,
knead until smooth. Shape dough into
14cm round; place on oiled oven tray.
Mark 1cm deep cross on top of dough;
brush with a little extra milk, sprinkle with
extra flour. Bake in moderately hot oven
25 minutes.
Best made on day of serving

Freeze Suitable

☺ FOR BABY Serve a small portion of
damper broken into tiny pieces

☺ FOR TODDLER Serve as above

*CHIVE AND
BACON DAMPER*

BEEF AND VEGETABLE HOTPOT

beef and vegetable hotpot

- **1 tablespoon olive oil**
- **500g beef strips**
- **1 medium (150g) brown onion, chopped coarsely**
- **1 medium (120g) zucchini, sliced thickly**
- **1 medium (200g) red capsicum, coarsely chopped**
- **¹/₂ cup (85g) coarsely chopped kumara**
- **1 trimmed (75g) celery stick, chopped coarsely**
- **125g button mushrooms, sliced thickly**
- **400g can tomatoes**
- **420g can baked beans**

Heat oil in large pan; cook beef, in batches, until browned. Add onion, cook stirring until onion is soft. Add zucchini, capsicum, kumara and celery, cook stirring 1 minute. Return beef and any juices to pan with mushrooms, undrained crushed tomatoes and baked beans. Bring to boil; simmer, covered, about 10 minutes or until vegetables are tender. Serve with mashed potato, if desired.

SERVES 4 TO 6

Storage Covered in refrigerator, up to 2 days
Freeze Suitable

☺ FOR BABY Puree to the desired consistency

☺ FOR TODDLER Chop to suit appropriate stage of development

☺ TIP For a variation, top each serve with a cheesy crouton. Sprinkle grated cheese and chopped parsley onto slices of French bread; grill until cheese melts.

creamy chicken soup

- **1 tablespoon olive oil**
- **1 medium (150g) brown onion, chopped finely**
- **1 clove garlic, crushed**
- **4 (440g) chicken thigh fillets, sliced thinly**
- **2 medium (240g) carrots, chopped coarsely**
- **2 trimmed (150g) celery sticks, chopped coarsely**
- **310g can creamed corn**
- **1 litre (4 cups) chicken stock**
- **1 cup (180g) short pasta (shells, elbow macaroni, etc)**
- **¹/₂ cup (125ml) cream**
- **1 tablespoon finely chopped fresh parsley**

Heat oil in large pan; cook onion and garlic, stirring until onion is soft. Add chicken, carrot, celery, corn and stock, bring to boil; simmer, covered, 20 minutes. Add pasta; simmer uncovered, about 20 minutes or until pasta is tender. Stir in cream; reheat without boiling, sprinkle with parsley to serve.

SERVES 4

Storage Covered in refrigerator, up to 2 days

☺ FOR BABY Puree to desired consistency

☺ FOR TODDLER Chop to suit appropriate stage of development

CREAMY CHICKEN SOUP

Heat oil in large pan; cook lamb, in batches, until browned all over. Add onion and garlic; cook, stirring, until onion is soft. Return lamb and any juices to pan with potato, carrot, eggplant, capsicum, leek, undrained crushed tomatoes, wine and herbs; simmer, covered, 1 hour. Add mushrooms; simmer, uncovered, 20 minutes or until lamb is tender and mixture thickens.

SERVES 4

Storage Covered , in refrigerator, up to 2 days
Freeze Suitable

☺ FOR BABY Puree with cooled boiled water, formula or breast milk to the desired consistency

☺ FOR TODDLER Chop to suit appropriate stage of development

home-style chicken casserole

- **1kg chicken pieces**
- **1 medium (150g) brown onion, sliced thinly**
- **125g button mushrooms, halved**
- **2 trimmed (150g) celery sticks, sliced thinly**
- **400g can tomatoes**
- **1 clove garlic, crushed**
- **1 teaspoon dried mixed herbs**
- **40g packet French onion soup mix**
- **1 cup (250ml) dry white wine**

Trim excess fat from chicken. Place chicken in oiled 3.5-litre (14-cup capacity) ovenproof dish with onion, mushrooms, celery, undrained crushed tomatoes, garlic and herbs; mix well. Pour combined soup mix and wine over chicken mixture; bake, uncovered, in moderate oven about 1 hour or until chicken is tender. Serve with steamed white rice.

SERVES 4 TO 6

Storage Covered, in refrigerator, up to 2 days
Freeze Suitable

☺ FOR BABY Remove chicken from bone; puree chicken and sauce with rice to the desired consistency; thin with cooled boiled water, if desired

☺ FOR TODDLER Remove chicken from bone; chop chicken and vegetables to suit appropriate stage of development; serve with rice, if desired

Mediterranean casserole

If fresh herbs are unavailable, substitute a half teaspoon each of dried thyme, oregano and basil leaves.

- **1 tablespoon olive oil**
- **1kg diced lamb**
- **1 medium (150g) brown onion, sliced thickly**
- **1 clove garlic, crushed**
- **6 small (240g) new potatoes, halved**
- **2 medium (240g) carrots, sliced thickly**
- **1 baby (60g) eggplant, sliced thinly**
- **1 medium (200g) red capsicum, sliced thickly**
- **1 medium (350g) leek, sliced thickly**
- **2 x 400g cans tomatoes**
- **1/2 cup (125ml) dry red wine**
- **2 teaspoons finely chopped fresh thyme**
- **2 teaspoons finely chopped fresh oregano**
- **2 teaspoons finely chopped fresh basil leaves**
- **125g button mushrooms, halved**

steak and kidney pie

1 lamb kidney
500g blade steak
plain flour
1 small (80g) brown onion,
   chopped finely
1 small (70g) carrot,
   chopped coarsely
1 trimmed (75g) celery stick,
   chopped coarsely
1/3 cup (55g) coarsely chopped
   sweet potato
1/2 cup 125ml) dry red wine
1/2 cup (125ml) water
1 sheet ready-rolled puff pastry
2 teaspoons milk

Remove skin and fat from kidney; halve
lengthways, remove and discard core
of fat. Rinse kidney under cold water;
pat dry. Cut kidney into thin slices; cut
beef into 2cm cubes. Toss kidney and
beef in flour; shake off excess. Combine
kidney, beef, vegetables, wine and water
in medium pan; bring to boil. Simmer,
covered, about 45 minutes or until beef
is tender.

Transfer filling mixture to oiled 23cm
pie plate; cool 10 minutes. Place pastry
over filling; trim to fit dish, brush with
milk. Decorate pie with pastry scraps,
make 2 small cuts in top; bake in hot oven
about 15 minutes or until browned.

SERVES 4 TO 6

Storage Covered, in refrigerator,
up to 2 days
Freeze Cooked filling suitable

☺ FOR BABY Puree filling with cooled
boiled water, breast milk or formula
to the desired consistency; blend with
pureed cooked potato

☺ FOR TODDLER Chop to suit
appropriate stage of development

☺ TIP Instead of pastry, top pie with
mashed potato sprinkled with combined
grated cheese and breadcrumbs.

OPPOSITE FROM TOP: MEDITERRANEAN
CASSEROLE, HOME-STYLE CHICKEN CASSEROLE
RIGHT: STEAK AND KIDNEY PIE

baked potato, ham and cheese omelette

4 medium (800g) potatoes
4 eggs
1/2 cup (70g) finely chopped leg ham
1 medium (190g) tomato, chopped finely
2 green onions, chopped finely
1 tablespoon finely chopped fresh parsley
1 cup (125g) coarsely grated cheddar cheese

Grate potatoes coarsely; using hand, squeeze out excess water. Beat eggs lightly in large bowl; add potato, ham, tomato, onion, parsley and half the cheese, mix well. Spread mixture into oiled shallow 1.5 litre (6-cup capacity) ovenproof dish; sprinkle with remaining cheese. Bake, uncovered, in moderate oven about 40 minutes or until browned.

SERVES 4

Storage Covered, in refrigerator, up to 2 days

☺ FOR BABY Puree a small quantity with boiled water, formula or breast milk to the desired consistency

☺ FOR TODDLER Serve as above

ABOVE FROM LEFT: BAKED POTATO, HAM AND CHEESE OMELETTE; GLAZED THAI CHICKEN

glazed Thai chicken

8 (1.2kg) chicken thigh fillets
2 teaspoons sweet chilli sauce
1 teaspoon fish sauce
2 teaspoons peanut oil
2 teaspoons chopped fresh coriander
1 tablespoon lime juice
2 teaspoons salt-reduced soy sauce

Trim excess fat from chicken; place chicken in large bowl with remaining ingredients. Cover, refrigerate 2 hours or overnight.

Cook chicken, in batches, on heated oiled griddle (or grill or barbecue) until browned all over and cooked through. Serve with salad, if desired.

SERVES 4 TO 6

Storage Covered, in refrigerator, up to 1 day
Freeze Uncooked marinated chicken suitable

☺ FOR BABY Unsuitable

☺ FOR TODDLER Serve as above, finely chopped, with mixed vegetables

mini burgers

500g minced beef
2 teaspoons tomato sauce
1 tablespoon teriyaki sauce
1 small (90g) brown onion, chopped finely
1 egg
6 small par-bake bread rolls
2 tablespoons tomato sauce, extra
6 cheese slices
2 small (120g) egg tomatoes, sliced thinly
6 small lettuce leaves

Using hand, combine mince, sauces, onion and egg in large bowl; shape into 12 patties. (Freeze 6 patties for later use.)

Cook patties on heated oiled griddle pan until cooked through.

Meanwhile, bake rolls according to manufacturer's instructions; split in half. Spread basis with extra sauce; top with patties then cheese. Grill until cheese melts; top with tomato, lettuce and remaining half of roll.

MAKES 6

Best assembled just before serving

Freeze Uncooked patties suitable

☺ FOR BABY Puree patties with cooled boiled water to the desired consistency

☺ FOR TODDLER Serve quartered

bright ideas for barbecuing

Toddlers love a family barbecue as much as everyone else and let's be honest – a 2 year old with a burger is considerably less worrying on the back lawn than on the dining room carpet!

• When adapting barbecue recipes for toddlers, reserve small portions of meat and flavour with simple marinades, such as salt-reduced soy sauce or honey. Thread onto bamboo skewers to cook (with fruit or vegies, if desired) but make sure skewer is removed before serving. For smaller babies, barbecued meat can be pureed or chopped finely.

• Toddlers also love cutlets, chicken drumsticks and small cobs of corn.

• Serve simple, accessible salads – lettuce, cherry tomatoes, blanched vegetable sticks, chunks of cheese, hard-boiled eggs or barbecued vegetables. Toddlers will happily pick their favourites.

• Food wrapped in bread is an easy way for a toddler to manage food outdoors. Avoid giving them big rolls or bread that is too thick – it's awkward to hold and eat. Instead try tortillas, Lebanese or pitta bread filled with small pieces of meat and salad. Mini-burgers and small steak sandwiches are also popular with toddlers.

• Sausages wrapped in fresh, buttered bread with tomato sauce (choose salt-reduced) are perennial favourites with toddlers and adults alike. As a change, try sausages wrapped in lavash with hummus. Smaller tots can have finely chopped skinless sausage alone or with their vegetables.

MINI BURGERS

pumpkin and kumara soup

- **1 tablespoon olive oil**
- **1 medium (150g) brown onion, chopped coarsely**
- **2 teaspoons finely grated fresh ginger**
- **1 green banana capsicum, seeded, chopped**
- **1 tablespoon finely chopped fresh lemon grass**
- **2 teaspoons ground cumin**
- **2 teaspoons ground coriander**
- **1 teaspoon ground turmeric**
- **500g trimmed pumpkin, chopped coarsely**
- **500g kumara, chopped coarsely**
- **1.5 litres (6 cups) chicken stock**
- **1/4 cup (60ml) coconut cream**

Heat oil in large pan; cook onion, stirring, until soft. Add ginger, capsicum, lemon grass, cumin, coriander and tumeric; cook, stirring, until fragrant. Add pumpkin and kumara; cook, stirring, 1 minute. Add stock, bring to boil; simmer, covered about 20 minutes or until vegetables are tender. Cool soup mixture 10 minutes; blend or process, in batches, until smooth.

Place soup in individual serving bowls, swirl with coconut cream; top with croutons, if desired.

SERVES 4 TO 6

PORK AND CHICKPEA CURRY

pork and chickpea curry

- **500g pork fillets**
- **1 large (200g) brown onion, sliced thinly**
- **1 tablespoon mild curry paste**
- **400g can tomatoes**
- **3/4 cup (180ml) vegetable stock**
- **300g can chickpeas, rinsed, drained**
- **1/2 cup (125ml) coconut milk**
- **300g spinach, trimmed**
- **2 teaspoons chopped fresh coriander leaves**

Cut pork into 2cm cubes; cook, uncovered, in large heated oiled pan, in batches, until well browned. Add onion and paste; cook, uncovered, until onion is soft. Return pork to pan; stir in undrained crushed tomatoes and stock. Bring to boil; simmer, covered, 45 minutes.

Stir in chickpeas, bring to boil; simmer, uncovered, stirring occasionally, about 15 minutes or until chickpeas are tender. Stir in milk, spinach and coriander; cook, stirring, until spinach is just wilted.

SERVES 4

Storage Covered, in refrigerator, up to 2 days
Freeze Suitable before adding coconut milk, spinach and coriander

☺ FOR BABY Unsuitable

☺ FOR TODDLER Serve as above, chopped finely

PUMPKIN AND KUMARA SOUP

Storage Covered, in refrigerator, up to 2 days
Freeze Suitable

☺ FOR BABY Puree with cooled boiled water to the desired consistency; serve without croutons

☺ FOR TODDLER Serve as above

roast scotch fillet with garlic rosemary potatoes

1.5kg piece beef scotch fillet
1 tablespoon olive oil
2 teaspoons cracked black pepper
5 medium (1kg) potatoes, quartered
2 cloves garlic, crushed
1 tablespoon fresh rosemary leaves
2 tablespoons olive oil, extra

Place beef on wire rack in baking dish, rub with oil then pepper; bake, uncovered, in hot oven 15 minutes. Remove from oven, reduce heat to moderate. Add combined potatoes, garlic, rosemary and extra oil to dish; bake, uncovered, about 45 minutes or until cooked as desired. Serve with seeded mustard and seasonal vegetables.

SERVES 4 TO 6

Best made just before serving

☺ FOR BABY Select beef without pepper, puree beef and vegetables with breast milk, formula or cooled boiled water to the desired consistency

☺ FOR TODDLER Select beef without pepper, chop beef and vegetables to suit appropriate stage of development

☺ TIP There is nothing better to tempt a toddler to eat their vegies than mixed roast vegetables. Use as wide a variety as possible to help introduce new flavours.

ROAST SCOTCH FILLET WITH GARLIC ROSEMARY POTATOES, TODDLER SERVE

ROAST SCOTCH FILLET WITH GARLIC ROSEMARY POTATOES

rack of lamb with orange couscous

**2 racks of lamb with
    8 cutlets each**
1/2 cup (125ml) orange juice
1/4 cup (60ml) redcurrant jelly
1/4 cup (60ml) dry white wine
**2 tablespoons finely chopped
    fresh chives**

ORANGE COUSCOUS
1 1/3 cups (330ml) orange juice
2 cloves
1 bay leaf
1/2 teaspoon ground cinnamon
1 1/2 cups (300g) couscous
30g butter

Place lamb on wire rack in baking dish; bake, uncovered, in moderately hot oven 35 minutes or until cooked as desired.

Meanwhile, combine juice, jelly, wine and chives in small pan; simmer, uncovered, until thickened slightly. Serve lamb with sauce and Orange Couscous.

Orange Couscous Combine juice, cloves, bay leaf and cinnamon in medium pan, bring to boil; remove from heat. Stir in couscous; stand about 3 minutes or until liquid is absorbed. Stir in chopped butter; discard cloves and bay leaf before serving.

SERVES 4

Best made just before serving

☺ FOR BABY Remove lamb from bone; puree lamb and couscous with cooled boiled water to the desired consistency

☺ FOR TODDLER Remove lamb from bone; chop to suit appropriate stage of development, serve with couscous

RACK OF LAMB WITH ORANGE COUSCOUS

lamb drumsticks

French-trimmed lamb shanks are called "drumsticks" by some butchers, the shanks having been trimmed of all sinew and fat so they resemble a gigantic chicken leg.

6 lamb drumsticks
1/2 cup (125ml) honey
1/4 cup (60ml) soy sauce
1 teaspoon French mustard

Make diagonal cuts, about 1cm apart, through to bone on both sides of shanks. Place in greased shallow ovenproof dish; pour over combined remaining ingredients. Cover, refrigerate 2 hours or overnight.

Bake, uncovered, in moderate oven about 40 minutes or until tender; brushing twice during cooking with pan juices.

Serve with cooked pasta and carrots, if desired.

SERVES 6

Storage Covered, in refrigerator, up to 2 days
Freeze Uncooked marinated lamb suitable

☺ FOR BABY Remove lamb from bone; puree lamb, pasta and carrots with cooled boiled water to the desired consistency

☺ FOR TODDLER Trim lamb drumstick to suit appropriate stage of development, serve with pasta and carrots

LAMB DRUMSTICKS, TODDLER SERVE

sunday roast

- **1.5kg chicken**
- **1 medium (150g) onion, sliced thickly**
- **1 medium (140g) lemon, sliced thickly**
- **2 teaspoons olive oil**
- **1 teaspoon salt**
- **4 medium (800g) potatoes, halved**
- **1kg pumpkin, cut into chunks**
- **2 medium (240g) onions, halved, extra**
- **2 medium (190g) tomatoes, halved**

MUSHROOM GRAVY

- **100g button mushrooms, sliced thinly**
- **1 tablespoon plain flour**
- **1/2 cup (125ml) white wine**
- **1/2 cup (125ml) chicken stock**

Wash chicken thoroughly; dry with absorbent paper. Place sliced onion and lemon inside cavity; secure opening with toothpick or skewer. Tie legs of chicken together with kitchen string; tuck wings under. Rub oil and salt all over chicken.

Place chicken, breast-side up, with potatoes, pumpkin and onion halves in oiled flameproof baking dish. Cover chicken with oiled foil; bake in moderate oven 45 minutes. Remove foil, add tomatoes; bake about 45 minutes or until chicken is cooked through and vegetables are tender. Serve with Mushroom Gravy.

Mushroom Gravy Transfer chicken and vegetables to serving dish. Cover to keep warm. Reserve 2 tablespoons of the pan juices, discarding extra fat. Heat juices and mushrooms in baking dish; stir in flour.

Cook, stirring, until mixture is well browned; gradually stir in combined wine and stock. Bring to boil; simmer, stirring, about 5 minutes or until gravy boils and thickens.

SERVES 4

Best made just before serving

☺ FOR BABY Puree chicken and vegetables separately with cooled boiled water to the desired consistency. Stir through a little gravy, if desired

☺ FOR TODDLER Remove chicken from bone; chop to suit appropriate stage of development, serve with accompaniments

SUNDAY ROAST, BABY SERVE

SUNDAY ROAST, TODDLER SERVE

SUNDAY ROAST

Storage Cover cooked Meatballs and Tomato Basil Sauce, separately; refrigerate up to 2 days

Freeze Uncooked meatballs suitable

☺ FOR BABY Puree small quantities of pasta and sauce with 1 meatball to the desired consistency

☺ FOR TODDLER Chop meatballs and spaghetti to suit appropriate stage of development

cheese souffle

2 tablespoons packaged breadcrumbs
60g butter
1/4 cup (40g) plain flour
1 cup (250ml) milk
1 cup (125g) coarsely grated cheddar cheese
3 eggs, separated

Oil four 1-cup (250ml-capacity) ovenproof dishes; sprinkle bases and sides with breadcrumbs, place on oven tray.

Melt butter in medium pan, add flour; cook, stirring, until mixture thickens and bubbles. Gradually stir in milk; stir until mixture boils and thickens. Remove from heat; stand 2 minutes, stir in cheese and egg yolks. Transfer mixture to large bowl, cover surface with plastic wrap; cool.

Beat egg whites in medium bowl with electric mixer until firm peaks form. Fold about a third of the egg whites into souffle mixture then fold in remainder. Divide mixture among prepared dishes; bake in hot oven about 20 minutes or until puffed and browned.

SERVES 4

Best made just before serving

☺ FOR BABY Puree to the desired consistency

☺ FOR TODDLER Serve as above, with salad, if desired

CHEESE SOUFFLE

ITALIAN MEATBALLS IN TOMATO BASIL SAUCE

Italian meatballs in tomato basil sauce

If fresh herbs are unavailable, substitute half a teaspoon each dried basil and mint.

500g pork and veal mince
1 medium (240g) zucchini, grated coarsely
1 medium (150g) onion, chopped finely
1 egg, beaten lightly
1/2 cup (35g) stale breadcrumbs
1/4 cup (60ml) tomato sauce
1 tablespoon finely chopped fresh basil leaves
1 tablespoon finely chopped fresh mint leaves
500g spaghetti
1/3 cup (25g) flaked parmesan cheese

TOMATO BASIL SAUCE
400g can tomatoes
410g can tomato puree
2 cloves garlic, crushed
1/4 cup finely chopped fresh basil leaves
1 teaspoon sugar

Combine mince, zucchini, onion, egg, breadcrumbs, sauce and herbs in medium bowl; mix well. Roll level tablespoons of mixture into balls. Place on oiled foil-lined oven tray; bake in moderately hot oven 25 minutes.

Meanwhile, cook spaghetti in large pan of boiling water, uncovered, until just tender; drain. Toss meatballs through sauce; serve over hot spaghetti and sprinkle with parmesan cheese.

Tomato Basil Sauce Combine undrained crushed tomatoes, puree, garlic, basil and sugar in medium pan; simmer, uncovered, about 15 minutes or until thickened.

pasta Siciliana

We used penne in this recipe but you can use any short pasta.

2 tablespoons olive oil
1 medium (150g) onion, chopped finely
1 clove garlic, crushed
2 medium (240g) zucchini, chopped coarsely
2 baby (120g) eggplants, sliced thickly
2 medium (380g) tomatoes, peeled, chopped
1 medium (200g) green capsicum, sliced thinly
400g can tomato puree
1/2 cup (125ml) dry red wine
1/4 teaspoon brown sugar
500g pasta
2 tablespoons finely chopped fresh basil leaves
1/2 cup (40g) finely grated parmesan cheese

Heat oil in large pan; cook onion and garlic, stirring, until onion is soft. Add zucchini, eggplant, tomato and capsicum; cook, stirring, until vegetables are tender. Stir in tomato puree, wine and sugar; simmer, uncovered, 5 minutes or until mixture thickens slightly.

Meanwhile, cook pasta in large pan of boiling water, uncovered, until just tender; drain. Toss sauce through pasta; sprinkle basil and cheese over pasta just before serving.

SERVES 4 TO 6

Storage Vegetable mixture, covered, in refrigerator up to 2 days

☺ FOR BABY Puree pasta and sauce (without basil and cheese) with cooled boiled water to the desired consistency

☺ FOR TODDLER Chop to suit appropriate stage of development

PASTA SICILIANA

BAKED BROADBEAN AND LEEK PASTA

baked broadbean and leek pasta

1 cup (180g) short pasta (shells, elbow macaroni, etc)
500g packet frozen broadbeans
100g butter
1 large (500g) leek, chopped coarsely
1/4 cup (35g) plain flour
1 litre (4 cups) milk
3/4 cup (90g) coarsely grated cheddar cheese
425g can tuna, drained, flaked
1 cup (70g) stale breadcrumbs

Cook pasta in large pan of boiling water, uncovered, until just tender; drain.

Boil, steam or microwave broadbeans until tender; drain. Refresh under cold water; then remove and discard outer skins. Melt half of the butter in large pan; cook leek, stirring, until tender. Combine leek mixture in large bowl with pasta and broadbeans.

Melt remaining butter in medium pan, add flour; cook, stirring, until mixture thickens and bubbles. Gradually stir in milk; stir until mixture boils and thickens, stir in half of the cheese. Combine cheese sauce and tuna in bowl with pasta and vegetables; mix well. Spoon pasta mixture into oiled 3-litre (12-cup capacity) ovenproof dish; sprinkle with combined breadcrumbs and remaining cheese. Bake, uncovered, in moderate oven about 20 minutes or until heated through and browned lightly.

SERVES 4 TO 6

Storage Covered, in refrigerator, up to 2 days
Freeze Suitable

☺ FOR BABY Puree with cooled boiled water to the desired consistency

☺ FOR TODDLER Chop to suit appropriate stage of development

pork and vegetable stir-fry

2 tablespoons vegetable oil
500g pork fillets, sliced thinly
1 medium (150g) onion,
  sliced thinly
1 clove garlic, crushed
1 medium (120g) carrot,
  sliced thinly
100g mushrooms, sliced thinly
150g green beans, halved
150g snow peas
1 cup (80g) bean sprouts
2 tablespoons oyster sauce
1 tablespoon plum sauce
1 tablespoon sherry

Heat half the oil in wok or large pan; stir-fry pork, in batches, until browned all over. Heat remaining oil in wok; stir-fry onion and garlic 1 minute. Add carrot, mushroom, and beans; stir-fry until vegetables are just tender. Return pork to pan with snow peas, sprouts, sauces and sherry; stir-fry until hot. Serve with steamed jasmine rice, if desired.

SERVES 4 TO 6

Best made just before serving

☺ FOR BABY Unsuitable

☺ FOR TODDLER Chop to suit appropriate stage of development

LEFT: PORK AND VEGETABLE STIR-FRY
BELOW: VEGETABLE LASAGNE

ATLANTIC SALMON WITH CITRUS BUTTER SAUCE

vegetable lasagne

- **1 tablespoon olive oil**
- **1 medium (150g) onion, chopped finely**
- **1 clove garlic, crushed**
- **2 medium (400g) red capsicums, chopped coarsely**
- **2 medium (120g) zucchini, sliced thinly**
- **2 baby (120g) eggplants, sliced thinly**
- **60g mushrooms, sliced thinly**
- **2 tablespoons tomato paste**
- **400g can tomatoes**
- **1/2 cup (125ml) dry white wine**
- **8 x 10cm x 16cm (200g) fresh lasagne sheets**
- **1/3 cup (25g) finely grated parmesan cheese**

WHITE SAUCE

- **60g butter**
- **1/4 cup (35g) plain flour**
- **2 cups (500ml) milk**
- **1/2 cup (60g) grated cheddar cheese**

Heat oil in large pan; cook onion and garlic, stirring, until onion is soft. Add capsicum, zucchini and eggplant; cook, stirring, until vegetables have softened.

Stir in mushrooms, tomato paste, undrained crushed tomatoes and wine; simmer, uncovered, about 15 minutes or until mixture thickens slightly.

Place 2 lasagne sheets over base of oiled 2-litre (8-cup capacity) ovenproof dish. Top with half the vegetable mixture and a third of the White Sauce. Repeat layering, using 3 lasagne sheets per layer, finishing with lasagne. Pour remaining White Sauce over lasagne; sprinkle with cheese. Bake, uncovered, in moderate oven about 40 minutes or until browned lightly and heated through. Serve with green salad, if desired.

White Sauce Melt butter in medium pan, add flour; cook, stirring, until mixture thickens and bubbles. Gradually add milk, stirring, until mixture boils and thickens; stir in cheese.

SERVES 4 TO 6

Storage Covered, in refrigerator, up to 2 days
Freeze Suitable

☺ FOR BABY Puree with cooled boiled water to the desired consistency

☺ FOR TODDLER Chop to suit appropriate stage of development

Atlantic salmon with citrus butter sauce

Lime rind and juice can be substituted for lemon in this recipe.

- **4 (880g) salmon cutlets**
- **60g butter**
- **2 teaspoons finely grated lemon rind**
- **2 tablespoons lemon juice**
- **1 tablespoon finely chopped fresh chives**
- **1/2 teaspoon cracked black pepper**

Cook salmon on heated oiled griddle (or grill or barbecue) until browned and cooked as desired; cover to keep warm. Combine remaining ingredients in small pan; cook, stirring, until butter is melted. Serve salmon drizzled with citrus butter sauce and mashed potato, if desired.

SERVES 4

Best made just before serving

☺ FOR BABY Omit pepper; puree salmon with cooled boiled water, and mashed potato if desired, to the desired consistency

☺ FOR TODDLER Omit pepper; chop salmon to suit appropriate stage of development, serve with mashed potato

baked orange cheesecake

200g plain sweet biscuits
125g butter, melted
2 eggs
1/3 cup (75g) sugar
250g packaged cream cheese
250g ricotta cheese
1 tablespoon orange rind,
** finely grated**
2 tablespoons orange juice

Line base of 20cm round springform tin with foil, grease base and side.

Process biscuits until crushed finely; add butter, process until just combined. Press biscuit mixture evenly over base and side of prepared tin, leaving 2cm border. Cover; refrigerate 1 hour.

Beat eggs and sugar in medium bowl with electric mixer until thick and creamy; add cheeses, rind and juice, beat cheese mixture until smooth.

Place springform tin on oven tray; pour cheese mixture into tin. Bake in moderate oven about 1 hour or until firm. Cool in oven with door ajar. Cover cheesecake; refrigerate 3 hours or overnight. Serve with orange segments, if desired.

SERVES 4 TO 6

Storage Refrigerate, covered, up to 3 days

☺ FOR BABY Older babies can eat filling if it is finely sieved

☺ FOR TODDLER Serve as above

citrus delicious

3 eggs, separated
¹/2 cup (110g) caster sugar
¹/2 cup (75g) self-raising flour
30g butter, melted
1 cup (250ml) milk
1 teaspoon grated orange rind
1 teaspoon grated lemon rind
¹/3 cup (80ml) lemon juice
¹/2 cup (110g) caster sugar, extra

Grease four 1-cup (250ml capacity) ovenproof dishes.

Beat egg yolks and sugar in medium bowl with electric mixer until thick and creamy; stir in sifted flour then butter, milk, rind, and juice.

Beat egg whites in small bowl with electric mixer until soft peaks form; gradually add extra sugar, beat until dissolved. Fold egg white mixture, in 2 batches, into lemon mixture; divide mixture among prepared dishes. Place dishes in large baking dish with enough boiling water to come halfway up sides; bake in moderate oven about 20 minutes or until set. Dust with icing sugar to serve, if desired.

SERVES 4

Best made just before serving

😊 FOR BABY Puree to the desired consistency

😊 FOR TODDLER Serve as above

pear and ricotta strudel

6 sheets fillo pastry
50g butter, melted
425g can pear halves, drained, sliced thickly
1 tablespoon flaked almonds

RICOTTA FILLING
1 cup (200g) ricotta cheese
¹/3 cup (25g) stale breadcrumbs
¹/4 cup (35g) finely chopped dried apricots
2 tablespoons finely chopped almonds, toasted
¹/4 cup (40g) icing sugar mixture
¹/2 teaspoon ground cinnamon

Brush each fillo sheet with butter; layer sheets on top of each other on buttered oven tray.

Spread filling 2cm from edge of 1 long side and 6cm from both ends; top with pears. Roll pastry to enclose filling, tucking in ends; position seam-side down, brush all over with remaining butter. Sprinkle with almonds; bake in moderate oven about 25 minutes or until browned lightly. Serve with cream, if desired.

Ricotta Filling Combine all ingredients in medium bowl; mix well.

SERVES 4

Best made just before serving

😊 FOR BABY Omit almonds; puree cooked filling mixture with cooled boiled water, breast milk or formula to the desired consistency

😊 FOR TODDLER Omit almonds; serve as above, with ice-cream, if desired

OPPOSITE FROM TOP: PEAR AND RICOTTA STRUDEL; BAKED ORANGE CHEESECAKE ABOVE: CITRUS DELICIOUS

BAKED BANANA SUNDAE

rhubarb and berry compote

¹/₂ cup (110g) caster sugar
1 cup (250ml) water
2 tablespoons lemon juice
3 cups (330g) coarsely chopped fresh rhubarb
250g strawberries, quartered
1 cup (150g) blueberries

Combine sugar, water and juice in medium pan; stir over heat, without boiling, until sugar dissolves. Add rhubarb; simmer, covered, 2 minutes or until just tender. Transfer to large bowl, stir in strawberries and blueberries; cool. Serve with cream, if desired.

SERVES 4 TO 6

Storage Covered, in refrigerator, up to 2 days

☺ FOR BABY Puree rhubarb to the desired consistency; stir through blended cereal, if desired

☺ FOR TODDLER Serve a small portion with cream or custard

baked banana sundae

60g butter
¹/₃ cup (75g) firmly packed brown sugar
8 small (700g) sugar bananas
1 litre chocolate ice-cream
150g fresh raspberries
8 wafer biscuits

CHOCOLATE FUDGE SAUCE
¹/₂ cup (125ml) cream
¹/₄ cup (55g) caster sugar
125g dark chocolate, chopped finely
1 teaspoon vanilla essence

Heat butter in large heavy-base pan; cook sugar, stirring, until dissolved. Add bananas; cook, turning occasionally, until just tender. Serve warm bananas with ice-cream, raspberries, wafers and Chocolate Fudge Sauce.

Chocolate Fudge Sauce Combine cream and sugar in small pan; cook over very low heat, stirring, until sugar is dissolved. Remove pan from heat; add chocolate and vanilla, stirring until chocolate melts. Serve sauce warm or cold.

SERVES 4 TO 6

Storage Chocolate Fudge Sauce can be made up to a week ahead; keep, covered, in refrigerator

☺ FOR BABY Puree cooked bananas to the desired consistency

☺ FOR TODDLERS Serve as above

RHUBARB AND BERRY COMPOTE

chocolate mousse

125g dark chocolate Melts
1 tablespoon orange juice
4 eggs, separated
300ml thickened cream

Stir chocolate, in small heatproof bowl over pan of simmering water, until melted, remove from heat; cool. Stir in juice then egg yolks; fold cream into chocolate mixture; transfer mixture to large bowl.

Beat egg whites in small bowl with electric mixer until soft peaks form. Fold egg whites into chocolate cream mixture, in 2 batches. Spoon mixture into serving dishes, cover; refrigerate 3 hours or overnight. Dust with cocoa and serve with strawberries, if desired.

SERVES 4 TO 6

Best made a day ahead

Storage Covered, in refrigerator, up to 2 days

☺ FOR BABY Unsuitable

☺ FOR TODDLER Serve as above

saucy butterscotch pudding

1 cup (150g) self-raising flour
1/2 cup (60g) almond meal
1/2 cup (100g) firmly packed
brown sugar
2/3 cup (160ml) milk
60g butter, melted
1 egg, beaten lightly

BUTTERSCOTCH SAUCE
1/2 cup (125ml) water
1 cup (250ml) cream
1/2 cup (125ml) golden syrup
40g butter

Grease 2-litre (8-cup capacity) ovenproof dish. Sift combined flour, meal and sugar into large bowl; add combined milk, butter and egg, stir until smooth. Pour mixture into prepared dish; pour hot Butterscotch Sauce carefully over pudding. Bake in moderate oven about 35 minutes or until pudding is firm. Serve with whipped cream, if desired.

Butterscotch Sauce Combine all ingredients in medium pan; cook, stirring, without boiling, about 2 minutes or until butter has melted.

SERVES 4

Best made just before serving

☺ FOR BABY Unsuitable

☺ FOR TODDLER Serve as above, with ice-cream, if desired.

CHOCOLATE MOUSSE

SAUCY BUTTERSCOTCH PUDDING

party food and birthday cakes

Although no one would argue that healthy food is best, when birthdays and parties come around it's wise to accept from the outset that the five food groups may take a bit of a battering. You don't have to turn the affair into one giant sugar fest either, but there's no need to panic at occasional over-indulgence. Children quickly learn to value a special celebration as much as we do and if "party food" is only associated with parties, then it's not going to interfere too much with everyday routine. Bear in mind as well that little ones are usually so excited by the fun of a party, they actually don't eat a great deal. Anyone who has ever cleaned up after a small child's party knows that birthday cake is usually messed about the plate and left – it's the candles and singing that form the unforgettable part of the experience. Only the adults ever seem to remember what flavour the cake was!

So don't get yourself in a twist making traffic-light sandwiches with tomato and cheese – no one has ever met a child who would eat one of these. On the other hand, there *are* ways of making party food slightly less unhealthy, without making it seem any less special or delicious and on the following pages you'll find lots of recipes and ideas. Don't think for a minute that you need to make *everything*. Choose one or two sweet things and a couple of savoury ones – and have fun!

noodle pancakes

Pancakes may be served hot or at room temperature. We used rice vermicelli for the noodles in this batter.

50g rice vermicelli
$1/4$ cup (35g) plain flour
I green onion, sliced finely
I clove garlic, crushed
I teaspoon grated fresh ginger
$1/2$ teaspoon ground coriander
2 tablespoons coconut milk
peanut oil, for shallow frying

Place noodles in small heatproof bowl, cover with boiling water; stand until just tender; drain. Cut noodles into 5cm lengths; combine in medium bowl with flour, onion, garlic, ginger, coriander and milk. Heat oil in large pan; shallow fry level tablespoons of mixture, in batches, until browned both sides and cooked through. Drain on absorbent paper;
serve with plum or sweet and sour sauce, if desired.

MAKES 12

Storage Best made just before serving

NOODLE PANCAKES

CHICKEN NUGGETS WITH OVEN-FRIED CHIPS

oven-fried chips

6 medium (1.2kg) potatoes
¼ cup (60ml) olive oil

Cut each potato lengthways in 1cm-wide strips; cut strips into 1cm chips. Boil, steam or microwave chips until just tender; drain on absorbent paper.

Combine chips and oil in single layer on oven tray; bake in very hot oven about 45 minutes or until crisp and brown.

MAKES 12 SERVINGS

Best made just before serving

chicken nuggets

1 slice white bread
170g single chicken breast fillet, chopped
¼ cup (30g) finely grated cheese
1 egg yolk
1 small (120g) potato, grated
1 small (80g) onion, grated
1 teaspoon chicken seasoning
1 teaspoon garlic salt
2 tablespoons packaged breadcrumbs
oil, for deep frying

Cut crust from bread, chop roughly. Blend or process bread, chicken and cheese until combined; transfer to medium bowl. Add egg, potato, onion and salt. Shape level tablespoons of mixture into nuggets; toss in breadcrumbs.

Deep fry nuggets, in batches, until chicken is cooked through and golden brown; drain on absorbent paper.

MAKES 16

Storage Covered, in refrigerator, up to 2 days
Freeze Uncooked nuggets suitable

funny-face sambos

Using a 8.5cm cutter, cut rounds from slices of bread. "Draw" food faces using the following toppings.

CARROT TOP grated carrot, green onion, tomato, parsley, cheese slice, cream cheese and chicken seasoning
LITTLE BOY cheese slice, Vegemite and tomato
PUSSY CAT peanut butter, sliced banana, lemon rind and raspberry jam
GRIZZLY BEAR Nutella, white chocolate Melts and red and white jelly beans

GRIZZLY BEAR

eggless chocolate cake

This cake is best eaten on the day it is made.

2 cups (300g) self-raising flour
¼ cup (25g) cocoa
½ cup (110g) caster sugar
1¼ cups (310ml) boiling water
2 tablespoons golden syrup
1 teaspoon bicarbonate of soda
90g butter, melted
1 teaspoon vanilla essence
½ cup (125ml) cream, whipped

CHOCOLATE FROSTING
2 tablespoons finely chopped dark chocolate
30g butter
¾ cup (120g) icing sugar mixture
1 tablespoon cocoa
1 tablespoon milk
½ teaspoon vanilla essence

Grease two 20cm round sandwich cake pans, line bases with baking paper. Sift flour, cocoa and sugar into medium bowl; whisk in combined water, syrup, soda, butter and essence.

Divide mixture between prepared pans; bake, uncovered, in moderately slow oven 25 minutes. Stand cakes 10 minutes; turn onto wire rack to cool. Sandwich cold cakes with whipped cream; top with Chocolate Frosting.

Chocolate Frosting Combine chocolate and butter in small pan; stir over low heat until chocolate is melted. Sift sugar and cocoa into small bowl; stir in chocolate mixture, milk and essence. Cover, refrigerate 15 minutes or until frosting thickens.

Freeze Un-iced cakes suitable

CARROT TOP

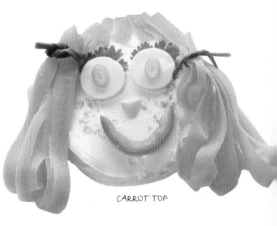

PUSSY CAT

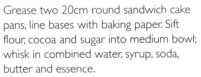

EGGLESS CHOCOLATE CAKE

LITTLE BOY

SPARKLING JUICE

sparkling juice

Pour equal parts of apple-blackcurrant or grape juice with soda or mineral water in a large jug; chill with ice cubes.

frankfurts

Place cocktail frankfurts in pan, cover with cold water; cook, uncovered, until water is just below boiling point, drain. Cut frankfurts into small pieces for very young children. A cute way to serve frankfurts to older children is to insert a pop stick into each cocktail frankfurt; serve with tomato sauce for dipping.

Alternatively, serve mini hot-dogs. Slice hot-dog rolls lengthways almost through; cut crossways into thirds. Place one cocktail frankfurt in each piece; top with tomato sauce and grated cheese.

FRANKFURTS

candied popcorn

2 tablespoons vegetable oil
1/2 cup (110g) popping corn
2 cups (440g) caster sugar
1 cup (250ml) water
1/2 teaspoon food colouring

Heat oil in large pan; cook corn, covered, shaking pan occasionally, until popping stops. Transfer to large bowl. Combine sugar, water and food colouring in medium heavy-base pan; stir over heat, without boiling, until sugar is dissolved. Bring to boil; boil, uncovered, about 15 minutes or until temperature reaches 154°C on candy thermometer (a teaspoon of mixture will crack when dropped into a cup of cold water). Allow bubbles to subside; add popcorn, stirring to coat with toffee mixture. When popcorn mixture has crystallised and separated, spread on foil-lined oven tray.

MAKES 6 CUPS

Storage Airtight container up to 3 days

SESAME CHICKEN MEATBALLS

monkey tails

5 (650g) firm sugar bananas, halved crossways
200g milk chocolate Melts
2 tablespoons vegetable oil
100s & 1000s, to decorate
coloured sprinkles, to decorate

Insert a pop stick into the base of each banana half. Melt chocolate in medium bowl over pan of simmering water; stir in oil. Dip bananas in chocolate mixture, one at a time, using a spoon to coat evenly. Decorate with 100s & 1000s and sprinkles, as desired. Place on tray; cover, refrigerate until set.

MAKES 10

sesame chicken meatballs

170g single chicken breast fillet, chopped
1/2 teaspoon fish sauce
1/2 teaspoon sweet chilli sauce
1 teaspoon lime juice
1 clove garlic, crushed
1 tablespoon shredded basil leaves
2 tablespoons sesame seeds
vegetable oil, for deep frying

Blend or process chicken, sauce, juice, garlic and leaves until almost smooth. Using hands, roll rounded teaspoons of chicken mixture into ball; roll ball in sesame seeds. Place on tray; repeat process with remaining mixture. Deep-fry chicken meatballs, in batches, until cooked through and browned lightly; drain on absorbent paper.

MAKES 18

MONKEY TAILS

CANDIED POPCORN

the party package

The type of party that you hold will naturally vary according to the age of the child, so when planning your party, always bear in mind the age of the guest of honour and what he or she is capable of.

As a general rule, toddlers do not need elaborate parties and although the accompanying adults might appreciate your hours of culinary efforts, the little ones will not. They tend to handle everything, take one or two bites and make an almighty mess – disheartening to the cook and entirely predictable!

Since parties are sociable occasions, by all means provide a snack for the adults, but keep the food for the 2 year olds very simple and try not to provide too much sugar. Excited toddlers can become very wound up after a sugary party – definite candidates for tears before bedtime!

Parties for 3 to 5 year olds really start to be fun, as the children excitedly anticipate the occasion and enjoy the idea of fancy dress and other theme parties. Involve the birthday child in the preparations as much as possible, such as designing an invitation that can then be photocopied and distributed, or helping to decorate hats or filling party bags. Enlist their opinion on the cake and party food as well, but remember that excitement will still rule the day and a great deal will not be eaten. Don't be too ambitious.

Food that is easy to handle and not too fussy is the sensible way to go, with a mix of both savoury and sweet things. Children also love to take a party bag away with them. This does not have to be another sugar hit – small, inexpensive toys and novelty items will be just as popular.

little green frogs

You need the ingredients listed on the packet of cake mix for this recipe.

340g packet Chocolate Buttercake cake mix
185g butter
2¼ cups (360g) icing sugar mixture
2 tablespoons milk
green food colouring
white marshmallows
Choc Bits
Smarties

Line 12-hole (⅓-cup/80ml-capacity) muffin pan with muffin cases. Make cake according to directions on packet; divide mixture among muffin cases. Bake in moderate oven 25 minutes; turn cakes onto wire rack to cool.

Meanwhile, beat softened butter in medium bowl with electric mixer until smooth and pale. With motor operating, gradually beat in icing sugar and milk; tint with food colouring.

Top cakes with frosting. Using a small knife, cut out a mouth shape from each cake. Decorate with marshmallows, Choc Bits and Smarties.

MAKES 12

Storage Airtight container up to 3 days
Freeze Un-iced cakes suitable

CHEESE TWISTS

cheese twists

I sheet ready-rolled puff pastry
I tablespoon tomato sauce
½ cup (60g) coarsely grated cheddar cheese
2 teaspoons milk

Cut pastry sheet in half. Spread one half with tomato sauce; sprinkle with cheese. Top with remaining pastry half; press down firmly.

Cut pastry into 12 strips; cut each strip in half. Twist strips then place, 2cm apart, on lightly oiled oven trays; brush with milk. Bake, uncovered, in hot oven about 10 minutes or until browned lightly. Serve warm or at room temperature.

MAKES 24

Storage Airtight container up to 2 days
Freeze Uncooked twists suitable

cassata cones

2 litres Neapolitan ice-cream
¼ cup (50g) green glace cherries, chopped
¼ cup (50g) red glace cherries, chopped
¼ cup (45g) dark Choc Bits, chopped
12 small square ice-cream cones
¼ cup (60ml) dark chocolate-flavoured ice-cream coating
¼ cup (60ml) white chocolate-flavoured ice-cream coating

CASSATA CONES

Place vanilla third of Neapolitan ice-cream in medium bowl. Using a slotted spoon, press down on ice-cream until just soft; add cherries and Choc Bits, stir until combined. Return ice-cream, covered, to freezer until set. Just before serving, place approximately 2 tablespoons of chocolate ice-cream in base of each cone. Next, place approximately 2 tablespoons of strawberry on top of chocolate then top with approximately 2 tablespoons of vanilla ice-cream mixture. Drizzle each cone with, first, dark chocolate then white chocolate ice-cream coating; serve immediately.

MAKES 12

LITTLE GREEN FROGS

chocolate crackles

1 cup (35g) rice bubbles
1/3 cup (55g) icing sugar mixture
1/4 cup (20g) desiccated coconut
2 teaspoons cocoa
60g Copha
sugar snowflakes, to decorate

Combine rice bubbles, sugar, coconut and cocoa in a large bowl. Heat Copha in small pan, uncovered, over low heat until melted; stir into dry ingredients, mix well. Spoon mixture into small paper patty cases; decorate with snowflakes. Refrigerate until set.

MAKES 18

Storage Airtight container, in refrigerator, up to 1 week

VEGETABLE ROSTI

vegetable rosti

15g butter
2 green onions, sliced thinly
1/2 cup (100g) coarsely grated kumara
1/2 cup (100g) coarsely grated potato
2 tablespoons finely chopped toasted pine nuts
1 egg yolk
2 tablespoons plain flour
2 tablespoons vegetable oil

Heat butter in medium pan; cook onion, kumara, potato and nuts, stirring, about 5 minutes or until potato is tender; cool. Stir in egg yolk and flour. Using floured hand, shape rounded teaspoons of mixture into balls; flatten slightly.

Heat oil in medium pan; shallow-fry rosti, in batches, until browned both sides and cooked through. Drain on absorbent paper; serve with plum or sweet and sour sauce, if desired.

MAKES 20

Storage Covered, in refrigerator, up to 2 days

CHOCOLATE CRACKLES

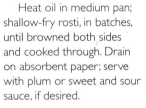

orange granita cups

4 medium (720g) oranges, halved
1/3 cup (80ml) cold water
3/4 cup (165ml) caster sugar
1/4 cup (60ml) light corn syrup
1 cup (250ml) warm water
2 egg whites, beaten lightly

Squeeze oranges, reserving the halves; strain and reserve juice (you need 2 cups [500ml] orange juice for this recipe). Scoop out and discard any remaining pulp from orange halves; reserve skin halves. Combine the cold water, sugar and syrup in small pan; heat, stirring, without boiling, until sugar dissolves. Simmer, uncovered, without stirring, 4 minutes. Stir in the warm water then the reserved juice. Pour mixture into shallow metal pan, cover with foil; freeze until just set. Working quickly, blend or process mixture with egg whites until smooth; scoop into orange skins, place on tray, return to freezer until set.

MAKES 8

ORANGE GRANITA CUPS

milk fruit log

1/3 cup (50g) finely chopped dried apricots
1/4 cup (40g) finely chopped seeded dates
1/2 cup (85g) raisins, finely chopped
2 teaspoons finely chopped red glace cherries
2 tablespoons boiling water
1/4 cup (50g) skim milk powder
1/2 cup (45g) desiccated coconut
1 teaspoon vanilla essence
1/2 cup (45g) desiccated coconut, extra

Combine apricots, dates, raisins and cherries in a medium mixing bowl. Pour the water into bowl, mix well; stand 10 minutes. Stir in milk powder, coconut and vanilla. Roll rounded teaspoons of mixture into balls; dip into extra coconut. Refrigerate until firm.

MAKES 25

Storage Airtight container, in refrigerator, up to 1 week

☺TIP Scissors make chopping dried fruit a breeze.

SULTANA CRUNCHIES

sultana crunchies

15g butter
1 tablespoon honey
1 tablespoon brown sugar
1 cup (30g) corn flakes
1/4 cup (40g) sultanas

Place 18 small paper patty cases on oven tray. Combine butter, honey and sugar in small pan; stir over heat until butter is melted. Add corn flakes and sultanas; mix gently, spoon mixture into patty cases. Bake, uncovered, in moderate oven about 10 minutes or until browned lightly.

MAKES 18

Storage Airtight container up to 1 week

rocky road

1/2 cup (45g) desiccated coconut
200g small multi-coloured marshmallows
1/2 cup (105g) mixed glace cherries, chopped finely
1/4 cup (35g) unsalted roasted peanuts, chopped finely
375g milk chocolate Melts, melted

Grease 20cm x 30cm lamington pan, cover base with baking paper. Combine coconut, marshmallows, cherries and peanuts in large bowl. Stir in chocolate; spread mixture into prepared pan. Cover; refrigerate 30 minutes or until set. Break into small pieces to serve.

Storage Airtight container, in refrigerator, up to 1 week

Delete nuts if serving to children under 5 years of age

FROM LEFT, MILK FRUIT LOG, ROCKY ROAD

One seagull

FOR THE CAKE:

340g packet Buttercake mix
25cm x 40cm prepared board
1 quantity Frosting (see page 113)
royal blue food colouring

TO DECORATE, YOU WILL NEED:

blue sugar crystals
4 plain wafer biscuits
6 small orange and yellow jube rings
20g packet spearmint Life Savers
pink, orange and yellow coloured sprinkles
green decorating gel
1 black licorice strap

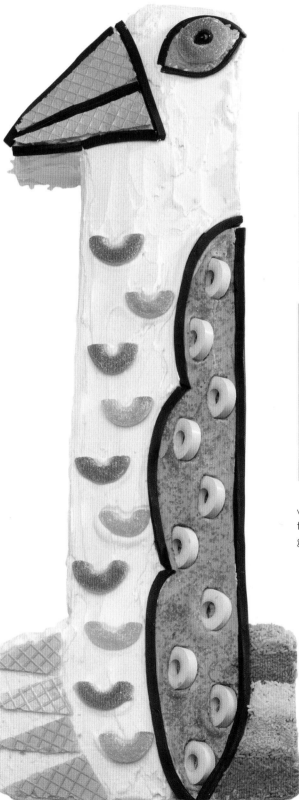

Grease two 8cm x 26cm bar cake pans, line bases with baking paper. Prepare cake according to directions on packet; divide mixture evenly between prepared pans. Bake in moderate oven about 35 minutes. Stand cakes in pans 5 minutes; turn onto wire racks to cool.

Leave one bar cake whole, cut the other into 3 pieces, as shown, in diagram 1. Assemble cake, as shown in diagram 2, on board to form the figure 1.

Reserve 3/4 frosting; tint remaining frosting blue. Spread bird's wing with blue and remainder of bird with white frosting. Sprinkle wing with blue sugar crystals. Cut wafers into triangles to form bird's beak and feet. Reserve one jube ring for eye; cut remaining jube rings in half. Push Life Savers halfway into wing and decorate body with jubes to resemble feathers.

Sprinkle pink, orange and yellow sprinkles in stripes along tail. Cut licorice strap into thin strips. Outline wing and beak with licorice. Use licorice to make shape of the eye, fill in with orange sprinkles; place jube in position, fill in hole with green decorating gel.

Taller at two!

FOR THE CAKE:

2 x 340g packets Buttercake mix
35cm x 45cm prepared board
2 quantities Frosting (see page 113)
orange food colouring
¼ cup (25g) cocoa

TO DECORATE, YOU WILL NEED:

1 black licorice strap
1 white marshmallow
1 green spiced berry
blue decorating gel
2 spearmint leaves
2 small grissini
2 small marshmallows
50g dark chocolate Melts, melted
yellow sugar crystals

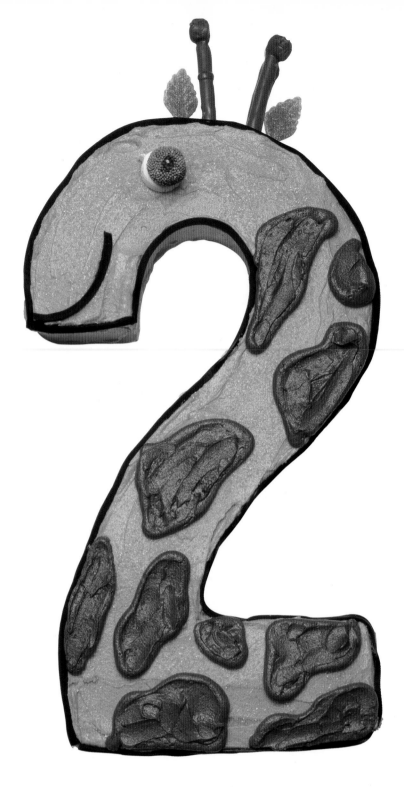

Grease 20cm x 30cm lamington pan and 8cm x 26cm bar cake pan, line bases with baking paper. Using both packets, prepare cakes according to directions on packet; pour into prepared pans. Bake in moderate oven about 25 minutes for bar pan and 40 minutes for lamington pan. Stand cakes in pans 5 minutes, turn onto wire racks to cool.

Cut out the figure 2 as shown above. Place cakes on prepared board.

Tint ¾ of frosting with orange colouring; tint remaining frosting by stirring in sifted cocoa.

Spread top and side of cake with orange frosting. Spoon chocolate frosting into piping bag fitted with a small plain tube; pipe spots onto cake. Cut licorice strap into thin strips. Position strips to outline cake and make mouth.

Cut marshmallow in half, discard one half; place spiced berry on top of remaining half. Pipe dot with blue gel on berry to complete eye; position on head. Insert toothpicks into base of spearmint leaves, position on head. Dip grissini and marshmallows in chocolate, place on baking paper-lined oven tray; stand until chocolate is set. Position grissini next to mint leaves to resemble horns. Sprinkle sugar crystals on orange frosting.

Fishes for three

FOR THE CAKE:

2 x 340g packets Buttercake mix
25cm x 40cm prepared board
2 quantities Frosting (see page 113)
royal blue food colouring

TO DECORATE, YOU WILL NEED:

4 peppermint Mentos
red decorating gel
4 apricot Roll-Ups
36 blue Smarties
5 ice-cream wafers
1 tablespoon orange coloured sprinkles
1 black licorice strap
2 teaspoons blue sugar crystals

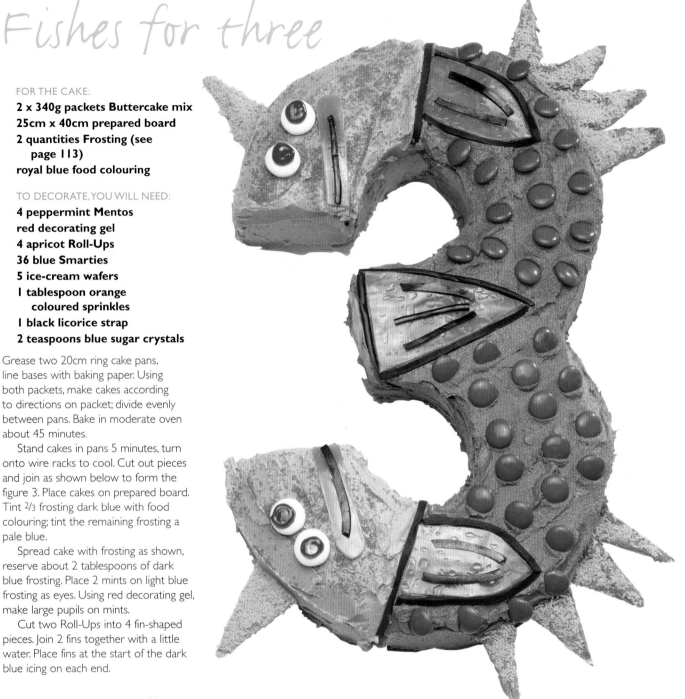

Grease two 20cm ring cake pans, line bases with baking paper. Using both packets, make cakes according to directions on packet; divide evenly between pans. Bake in moderate oven about 45 minutes.

Stand cakes in pans 5 minutes, turn onto wire racks to cool. Cut out pieces and join as shown below to form the figure 3. Place cakes on prepared board. Tint 2/3 frosting dark blue with food colouring; tint the remaining frosting a pale blue.

Spread cake with frosting as shown, reserve about 2 tablespoons of dark blue frosting. Place 2 mints on light blue frosting as eyes. Using red decorating gel, make large pupils on mints.

Cut two Roll-Ups into 4 fin-shaped pieces. Join 2 fins together with a little water. Place fins at the start of the dark blue icing on each end.

Cut two 5cm x 9cm triangles from Roll-Ups. Join triangles together with a little water. Place on cake at the centre of the figure 3 to resemble a tail.

Cut four 1cm x 6cm strips from remaining Roll-Ups, shape one end into a curve; join two pieces with a little water. Place Roll-Ups on each end to resemble a mouth. Place Smarties on cake to resemble scales. Cut wafers in half diagonally.

Place 8 pieces of wafer on top and bottom outer edge of cake, as shown, to form spines. Place 2 remaining wafer pieces on side of cake above eyes. Spread wafers with reserved frosting. Sprinkle wafer spines with orange sprinkles.

Cut licorice into thin pieces. Outline fins, tail and join of frostings; define fins, tail and mouth with licorice strips. Sprinkle pale blue heads with blue sugar crystals.

Tiger turns four

FOR THE CAKE:

340g packet Buttercake mix
30cm x 40cm prepared board
2 quantities frosting (see page 113)
yellow food colouring

TO DECORATE, YOU WILL NEED:

1 black licorice strap
green decorating gel
2 pink Smarties
2 x 5cm iced biscuits
4 pieces spaghetti
100g milk chocolate Melts
red decorating gel
6 peppermint Tic Tacs
15cm strip red Fruity Metres
2 vanilla ice-cream wafers

Grease 20cm x 30cm lamington pan, line base with baking paper. Prepare cake mix according to directions on packet; pour into prepared pan. Bake in moderate oven about 25 minutes. Stand cake in pan 5 minutes; turn onto wire rack to cool.

Cut cake into 3 equal pieces lengthways. Cut 2 pieces into 3 sections each, as shown in diagram 1. Assemble pieces on prepared board to make the figure 4, as shown in diagram 2. Tint frosting with yellow food colouring. Spread frosting over top and side of cake, fluff frosting with a fork to resemble fur.

Cut licorice strap into thin strips; position strips to outline eyebrows, eyes and mouth. Pipe green gel to complete eyebrows. Place Smarties on cake to form eyes; dot with green gel to complete.

Cut slice off each biscuit, discard small piece; place larger biscuit shapes on cake to form cheeks, outline with licorice. Make whiskers by breaking spaghetti pieces in half; roll in melted chocolate to coat, place on baking paper, allow to set. Place spaghetti whiskers in position; spread red gel over nose to complete, use Tic Tacs to form teeth.

Cut Fruity Metres into 3 triangles; position on head to form "fringe".

Cut each wafer into 4cm circle. Pipe red gel over wafers, press into top of cake, place licorice strip on each ear to complete.

FOR THE CAKE:

340g packet Buttercake mix
25cm x 35cm prepared board
2 quantities Frosting (see below)
pink, green, black, blue and
   orange food colourings

TO DECORATE, YOU WILL NEED:

thin red licorice rope
1 black licorice strap
15g packet peppermint Tic Tacs
2 peppermint Mentos
blue decorating gel
2 small yellow banana lollies
2 green spiced berries

Grease 20cm ring cake pan and 8cm x 26cm bar cake pan, line bases with baking paper. Using both packets, prepare cake mix according to directions on packet, divide mixture between pans. Bake in moderate oven about 25 minutes. Stand cake in pans 5 minutes, turn onto wire racks to cool.

Cut out cake to form the figure 5 as shown in diagram 1. Assemble pieces on prepared board, as shown in diagram 2. Tint 1/2 frosting with pink colouring, 1/4 with green colouring, and a 1/4 cup of remaining frosting with black colouring. Of remaining frosting, tint 1/3 with blue colouring and remaining frosting with orange colouring.

Spread top and outer side of round cake with pink frosting. With remaining green frosting, make a 2cm border on inside edge of round cake, and on top of cake to form mouth. Spread bar cake top and sides with orange frosting and eye area with black frosting. Spoon remaining green frosting into piping bag fitted with a small plain tube; pipe below black for nose.

Spoon blue frosting into clean piping bag fitted with a small plain tube, pipe 6 lines dividing pink and orange frostings. Cut black licorice strap into thin strips. Position red licorice rope to outline mouth and black licorice strips to outline eyes.

Cut remaining black licorice strips into small pieces to make whiskers. Arrange Tic Tacs to form teeth. Dot Mentos with blue gel to form eyes; place bananas above eyes for eyebrows and spiced berries for ears.

Gotcha! at five

FROSTING

125g soft butter
1 1/2 cups (240g) icing
   sugar mixture
2 tablespoons milk

Beat butter in small bowl with electric mixer until light in colour; gradually beat in half the sugar, then the milk, then the remaining sugar. Flavour and colour frosting as desired.

Preparing cake boards To make a cake easy to handle as well as more attractive, place it on a board which has been covered in decorative paper. We've given approximate cake board size with each recipe. Using masonite or a similarly strong board, cut your paper 5cm to 10cm larger than the shaped board.

glossary

UNPROCESSED BRAN

BLENDED CEREAL

SEMOLINA

APPLE-BLACKCURRANT JUICE

a sweetened drink made from these two fruits, sweetener and water, with vitamin supplements.

AGNOLOTTI fresh crescent- or rectangular-shaped filled pasta.

ALMOND MEAL blanched ground almonds.

ANCHOVETTE a paste made from fish, wheat flour, salt, flavour and colouring. Also known as fish paste.

BACON RASHERS also known as slices of bacon; made from pork side, cured and smoked. **Streaky bacon** is the fatty end of a bacon rasher (slice), without the lean (eye) meat.

BANANA CHILLI a mild yellow/green banana-shaped chilli. Also known as sweet banana peppers. Seeds and membranes should be discarded before use.

BEANS

3-Bean mix a canned mix of red kidney, green lima and great northern beans.

4-Bean mix a canned mix of red kidney, garbanzo, baby lima and butter beans.

BEAN SPROUTS also known as bean shoots; tender new growths of assorted beans and seeds germinated for consumption as sprouts. The most readily available are mung bean, soy bean, alfalfa and snow pea sprouts.

BEEF

Blade steak from the shoulder blade area.

Corned beef cut from the brisket or silverside cured in a piquantly flavoured brine.

Minced also known as ground beef or hamburger.

Scotch fillet eye of the rib roast; rib-eye roll; cube roll.

BICARBONATE OF SODA also known as baking soda.

BLANCHING to partially cook food (usually vegetables and fruits) very briefly, in boiling water; then draining and plunging into cold water.

BREADCRUMBS

Packaged fine-textured, crunchy, purchased, white breadcrumbs.

DARK CHOCOLATE

MILK CHOCOLATE MELTS

WHITE CHOCOLATE MELTS

DARK CHOC BITS

DARK CHOCOLATE MELTS

Stale 1- or 2-day-old bread made into crumbs by grating or blending.

BUTTER use salted or unsalted ("sweet") butter; 125g is equal to 1 stick butter.

CAPSICUM

also known as bell pepper or, simply, pepper. Seeds and membranes should be discarded before use.

CEREALS

Blended cereal recommended first food for babies from 4 months. A dry mixture of ground rice, maize flour, soy flour, various vitamins and minerals.

Bran flakes a breakfast cereal based on processed wheat bran enriched with vitamins.

Bran, unprocessed made from the outer layer of a cereal, most often the husks of wheat, rice or oats.

Breakfast biscuits made from wholewheat, salt, sugar, malt extract and various vitamins and minerals. Commonly known as Weet-Bix or Shredded Wheat.

Corn flakes breakfast cereal made from toasted corn.

Muesli/granola breakfast cereal made from a mixture of raw or toasted grains, dried fruit, nuts, coconut and sugar.

Rice bubbles breakfast cereal made from puffed rice, sugar, salt and malt extract, plus added vitamins and minerals.

Rolled oats/oatmeal whole oats grains steamed, rolled and flattened; used for making porridge or in baking.

Semolina made from durum wheat milled into various textured granules, all of these finer than flour. Used to make couscous, good pastas, some kinds of gnocchi and many Middle-Eastern and Indian sweets.

CHICKPEAS also called garbanzos, hummus or channa; an irregularly round, sandy-coloured legume used extensively in Mediterranean, Hispanic and Indian cooking.

CHOCOLATE

Choc Bits also known as chocolate chips and chocolate morsels; available in milk, white and dark chocolate. Made of cocoa liquor, cocoa butter, sugar and an emulsifier, these hold their shape in baking and are ideal when used for decorating.

Cocoa cocoa powder.

Dark eating-quality chocolate; made of cocoa liquor, cocoa butter and sugar.

Melts available in milk, white and dark chocolate. Made of sugar, vegetable fats, milk solids, cocoa powder, butter oil and emulsifiers, these are good for melting and moulding.

CINNAMON SUGAR

combination of caster sugar and ground cinnamon.

COCONUT

Cream available in cans and cartons; made from coconut and water.

Desiccated unsweetened, concentrated, dried and shredded coconut.

Milk pure, unsweetened coconut milk available in cans and cartons.

BREAKFAST BISCUITS

CORN FLAKES

ROLLED OATS

BRAN FLAKES

MUESLI

RICE BUBBLES

KIWI FRUIT

COLESLAW DRESSING
commercially prepared
mayonnaise-style dressing
commonly used in cabbage
and some fruit salads. Contains
oil, sugar, vinegar, egg yolk, salt,
cornflour, spices and skim
milk powder.

COPHA a solid white shortening
based on coconut oil. Kremelta
and Palmin can be substituted.

CORNFLOUR also known as
cornstarch; used as a thickening
agent in cooking.

CORN SYRUP a thick sweet
syrup available in light or dark
colour, either can be substituted
for the other; glucose syrup (liquid
glucose) can be substituted.

COUSCOUS a fine, grain-
like cereal product originating
in North Africa; made from
semolina rolled into balls.

CREAM

Fresh (minimum fat content
35%) also known as pouring
cream; has no additives like
commercially thickened cream.

Sour (minimum fat content 35%)
a thick, commercially-cultured
soured cream good for dips,
toppings and baked cheesecakes.

Thickened (minimum fat
content 35%) a whipping cream
containing a thickener.

CURRY POWDER a blend of
ground, powdered spices used
for convenience when making
Indian food. Can consist of
some or all of the following
spices in varying proportions:
dried chilli, cinnamon, coriander,
cumin, fennel, fenugreek, mace,
cardamom and turmeric.

DAMPER originally, unleavened
bread cooked in the ashen coals
of a campfire; today, available in
loaf and mini sizes enriched with
butter and milk.

EGGPLANT also known as
aubergine.

ESSENCES also known as
extracts; generally the byproduct
of distillation of plants.

FILLO PASTRY also known as
phyllo; tissue-thin pastry sheets
purchased chilled or frozen that
are easy to work with and very
versatile, lending themselves to
both sweet and savoury dishes.

FISH FILLETS fish pieces that
have been boned and skinned.

FLOUR

Plain an all-purpose flour, made
from wheat.

Rice a very fine flour, made from
ground white rice.

Self-raising plain flour sifted with
baking powder in the proportion
of 1 cup flour to 2 teaspoons
baking powder.

Wholemeal plain also known as
all-purpose wholewheat flour, has
no baking powder added.

FOOD COLOURINGS
available in liquid, powdered and
concentrated paste forms.

FRANKFURT

Cocktail a lightly smoked pre-
cooked sausage made from a
mixture of pork, beef or veal,
starch, salt and various additives
in red casing. Usually about 6cm
in length.

Continental a fine-textured
smoked pre-cooked sausage
made from a mixture of pork,
beef and veal, selected spices,
starch, salt and various additives
in red casing. Usually about
15cm in length.

FRENCH ONION SOUP MIX
a packaged soup mix often added
to meat and poultry dishes for
flavour and as a thickening agent.

GELATINE (gelatin) we used
powdered gelatine. It is also
available in sheet form known
as leaf gelatine.

GHERKIN sometimes known
as a cornichon; young,
dark-green, extremely
tiny cucumbers grown
especially for pickling.

GNOCCHI Italian
"dumplings" made of

potatoes, semolina or flour; can
be cooked in boiling water or
baked with a sauce.

GOLDEN SYRUP a byproduct
of refined sugarcane; pure maple
syrup, corn syrup or honey can
be substituted.

GRAVOX a pre-mixed powder
containing wheat flour, salt,
caramel colouring and flavouring;
used to make gravy.

GRISSINI crisp, extremely long
and thin Italian breadsticks.

**HUNDREDS AND
THOUSANDS** nonpareils.

ICE MAGIC

Chocolate chocolate-flavoured
ice-cream coating made of
vegetable oils, sugar, cocoa, skim
milk powder and emulsifiers.

White white chocolate-flavoured
ice-cream coating made of
vegetable fat, sugar, milk solids,
lactose, emulsifiers and flavours.

JELLY CRYSTALS fruit-flavoured
gelatine crystals available from
supermarkets; known frequently
by the brand name Jello, which
has become generic.

KIWI FRUIT also known as
Chinese gooseberry.

KUMARA Polynesian name of
orange-fleshed sweet potato
often incorrectly called a yam.

LAMB

Cutlet small, tender rib chop.

Diced cubed lean meat.

Forequarter chop medium-sized
chop cut from the shoulder.

Minced ground lamb.

Rack row of cutlets.

Shank forequarter leg.

LAVASH BREAD flat, unleavened
bread of Mediterranean origin.

LENTILS, RED a small dried red/
orange pulse originating in
the Middle East.

**MEXICAN-STYLE CHILLI
POWDER** a blend of ground
chilli, cumin, oregano and garlic.
Used in cooking to impart a
Mexican-like flavour to food.

MILK

Condensed canned, milk of thick
consistency which has been
evaporated and sweetened.

Formula a formulated breast milk
substitute sold in powdered form.

Skim Milk Powder we used
dried milk powder having 1%
fat content when dry and 0.1%
when reconstituted.

MIXED DRIED FRUIT
a combination of sultanas, raisins,
currants, mixed peel and cherries.

MUFFIN, ENGLISH a round, flat
yeast cake, baked on both sides;
often confused with the batter-
based crumpet.

NEAPOLITAN ICE-CREAM
a widely available, commercially
prepared, 3-flavour combination
ice-cream. Usually strawberry,
vanilla and chocolate.

NOODLES

Bean thread also called
cellophane; made from green
mung bean flour. Good softened
in soups and salads or deep-fried
with vegetables.

Instant Also known as ramen,
a crinkly or straight dried wheat
noodle. Are referred to as
2-minute noodles in reference
to their short cooking time.

Rice vermicelli also known as
rice-flour or rice-stick noodles;
made from ground rice. Sold
dried, they are best either deep-
fried or soaked then stir-fried or
used in soups.

NUTELLA commercially made
chocolate hazelnut spread.

OLIVE OIL

Extra virgin and virgin the
highest quality olive oils, obtained
from the first pressings of
the olives.

Olive mono-unsaturated; made
from the pressing of tree-
ripened olives. Especially good
for everyday cooking and as an
ingredient. Extra Light or Light
describes the mild flavour, not the
fat levels.

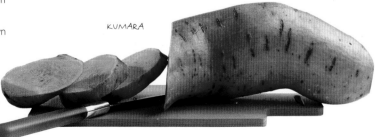

KUMARA

RED ONION

GREEN ONION

BROWN ONION

Peanut pressed from ground peanuts; most commonly used oil in Asian cooking because of its high smoke point.

Sesame made from roasted, crushed, white sesame seeds; used as a flavouring rather than a cooking medium.

Vegetable any of a number of cooking oils having a plant rather than animal source.

ONION

Brown large brown-skinned onion with strong flavour.

Green also known as scallion or (incorrectly) shallot; an immature onion picked before the bulb has fully formed, having a long, bright-green edible stalk.

Red also known as Spanish, red Spanish or Bermuda onion; a sweet-flavoured, large, purple-red onion that is particularly good eaten raw in salads.

PAPPADUMS sun-dried wafers made from a combination of lentil and rice flours, oil and spices; can be deep-fried or "puffed" in the microwave oven.

PAR-BAKE BREAD ROLLS also known as "bake at home" bread rolls. Commercially baked bread rolls that have been cooked to 80% of total cooking time.

PINE NUT also known as pignoli; small, cream-coloured kernels obtained from the cones of different varieties of pine trees.

PLAIN SWEET BISCUITS uniced, plain, packaged biscuit, sometimes sprinkled with sugar.

POLENTA a flour-like cereal made of ground corn (maize); similar to cornmeal but coarser and darker in colour; also the name of the dish made from it.

POPPING CORN dried kernels of a particular strain of corn which pop when heated.

PORK

Fillet skinless, boneless eye-fillet cut from the loin.

PORK & VEAL MINCE

a combination of pork and veal coarsely ground together.

REDCURRANT JELLY a

preserve made from redcurrants used as a glaze for desserts and meats or as a part of a sauce.

RICE

Calrose a medium-grain rice that is extremely versatile; can substitute for short- or long-grain rice if necessary.

Paper mostly from Vietnam (banh trang). Made from a paste of ground rice and water and stamped into rounds, with a woven pattern. Dipped briefly in water, they become pliable wrappers for fried food and for eating fresh vegetables.

SATAY MARINADE

commercially prepared thin version of the traditional mixture of peanuts, sugar, soy sauce, salt, garlic, chilli, spices and vinegar.

SAUCES

Barbecue spicy tomato-based sauce used to marinate, baste or as an accompaniment.

Fish also called nam pla or nuoc nam; made from pulverised salted fermented fish, most often anchovies. Has a pungent smell and strong taste; use sparingly. There are many kinds, each of varying intensity.

Hoisin thick, sweet and spicy Chinese paste made from salted fermented soy beans, onions and garlic; used as a marinade or to baste, or to accent stir-fries and barbecued or roasted foods.

Oyster Asian in origin, this rich, brown sauce is made from oysters and their brine, cooked with salt and soy sauce, and thickened with starches.

Plum thick, sweet and sour dipping sauce made from plums, vinegar, sugar, chillies and spices.

Soy made from fermented soy beans. Several variations are available in most supermarkets and Asian food stores. We used a sauce with 46% of the salt removed after manufacture.

Sweet chilli mild, Thai-type sauce made from red chillies, sugar, garlic and vinegar.

Teriyaki homemade or commercially bottled sauce usually made from soy sauce, corn syrup, vinegar, ginger and other spices; it imparts a distinctive glaze when brushed on grilled meats.

Tomato also known as ketchup or catsup; a flavoured condiment made from tomatoes, vinegar and spices.

Worcestershire thin, dark-brown spicy sauce used as a seasoning for meat, gravies and cocktails and as a condiment.

SCONES also known as biscuits.

SPONGE-FINGER BISCUITS

also known as Savoiardi, Savoy biscuits or ladyfingers. They are Italian-style crisp biscuits made from a sponge-cake mixture.

SPRING ROLL WRAPPERS

are also sometimes called egg roll wrappers; they come in various sizes and can be purchased fresh or frozen from Asian supermarkets. Made from a delicate wheat-based pastry, they can be used for making gow gee, samosas and spring rolls.

STOCK I cup (250ml) stock is the equivalent of I cup (250ml) water plus I crumbled stock cube (or I teaspoon stock powder).

SUGAR we used coarse, granulated table sugar, also known as crystal sugar, unless otherwise specified.

Brown an extremely soft, fine granulated sugar retaining its molasses flavour.

Caster also known as superfine or finely granulated table sugar.

Icing sugar mixture also known as confectioners' sugar or powdered sugar; granulated sugar crushed together with a small amount (about 3%) cornflour added.

SULTANAS golden raisins.

TAHINI a rich, buttery paste made from crushed sesame seeds; used in making hummus and other Middle-Eastern sauces.

TOMATO PASTE triple-concentrated tomato puree used to flavour soups, stews, sauces and casseroles.

TORTELLINI small rounds of pasta, filled, sealed, then shaped into rounds.

TORTILLA thin, round unleavened bread originating in Mexico; some are made from wheat flour and others from corn (maizemeal). Also, the Spanish word for a thick omelette, usually containing potatoes.

VEGEMITE yeast extract spread; Marmite or Promite can be substituted.

ZUCCHINI also known as courgette.

BEAN THREAD NOODLES

RICE VERMICELLI

INSTANT NOODLES

conversion chart

MEASURES

One Australian metric measuring cup holds approximately 250ml; one Australian metric tablespoon holds 20ml; one Australian metric teaspoon holds 5ml.

The difference between one country's measuring cups and another's is within a two- or three-teaspoon variance, and will not affect your cooking results. North America, New Zealand and the United Kingdom use a 15ml tablespoon.

All cup and spoon measurements are level. The most accurate way of measuring dry ingredients is to weigh them. When measuring liquids, use a clear glass or plastic jug with the metric markings.

We use large eggs with an average weight of 60g.

DRY MEASURES

METRIC	IMPERIAL
15g	½oz
30g	1oz
60g	2oz
90g	3oz
125g	4oz (¼lb)
155g	5oz
185g	6oz
220g	7oz
250g	8oz (½lb)
280g	9oz
315g	10oz
345g	11oz
375g	12oz (¾lb)
410g	13oz
440g	14oz
470g	15oz
500g	16oz (1lb)
750g	24oz (1½lb)
1kg	32oz (2lb)

LIQUID MEASURES

METRIC	IMPERIAL
30ml	1 fluid oz
60ml	2 fluid oz
100ml	3 fluid oz
125ml	4 fluid oz
150ml	5 fluid oz (¼ pint/1 gill)
190ml	6 fluid oz
250ml	8 fluid oz
300ml	10 fluid oz (½ pint)
500ml	16 fluid oz
600ml	20 fluid oz (1 pint)
1000ml (1 litre)	1¾ pints

LENGTH MEASURES

METRIC	IMPERIAL
3mm	⅛in
6mm	¼in
1cm	½in
2cm	¾in
2.5cm	1in
5cm	2in
6cm	2½in
8cm	3in
10cm	4in
13cm	5in
15cm	6in
18cm	7in
20cm	8in
23cm	9in
25cm	10in
28cm	11in
30cm	12in (1ft)

OVEN TEMPERATURES

These oven temperatures are only a guide for conventional ovens. For fan-forced ovens, check the manufacturer's manual.

	°C (CELSIUS)	°F (FAHRENHEIT)	GAS MARK
Very slow	120	250	½
Slow	150	275-300	1-2
Moderately slow	160	325	3
Moderate	180	350-375	4-5
Moderately hot	200	400	6
Hot	220	425-450	7-8
Very hot	240	475	9

index

ARE YOU MISSING SOME COOKBOOKS?

The Australian Women's Weekly Cookbooks are available from bookshops, cookshops, supermarkets and other stores all over the world. You can also buy direct from the publisher, using the order form below.

TITLE	RRP	QTY
100 Fast Fillets	£6.99	
A Taste of Chocolate	£6.99	
After Work Fast	£6.99	
Beginners Cooking Class	£6.99	
Beginners Simple Meals	£6.99	
Beginners Thai	£6.99	
Best Food Fast	£6.99	
Breads & Muffins	£6.99	
Brunches, Lunches & Treats	£6.99	
Cafe Classics	£6.99	
Cafe Favourites	£6.99	
Cakes Bakes & Desserts	£6.99	
Cakes Biscuits & Slices	£6.99	
Cakes Cooking Class	£6.99	
Caribbean Cooking	£6.99	
Casseroles	£6.99	
Casseroles & Slow-Cooked Classics	£6.99	
Cheap Eats	£6.99	
Cheesecakes: baked and chilled	£6.99	
Chicken	£6.99	
Chinese and the foods of Thailand, Vietnam, Malaysia & Japan	£6.99	
Chinese Cooking Class	£6.99	
Chocs & Treats	£6.99	
Cookies & Biscuits	£6.99	
Cooking Class Cake Decorating	£6.99	
Cupcakes & Fairycakes	£6.99	
Detox	£6.99	
Dinner Lamb	£6.99	
Dinner Seafood	£6.99	
Easy Comfort Food	£6.99	
Easy Curry	£6.99	
Easy Midweek Meals	£6.99	
Easy Spanish-Style	£6.99	
Food for Fit and Healthy Kids	£6.99	
Foods of the Mediterranean	£6.99	
Foods That Fight Back	£6.99	
Fresh Food Fast	£6.99	
Fresh Food for Babies & Toddlers	£6.99	
Good Food for Babies & Toddlers	£6.99	
Great Kids' Cakes	£6.99	
Greek Cooking Class	£6.99	
Grills	£6.99	
Healthy Heart Cookbook	£6.99	
Indian Cooking Class	£6.99	
Japanese Cooking Class	£6.99	

TITLE	RRP	QTY
Just For One	£6.99	
Just For Two	£6.99	
Kids' Birthday Cakes	£6.99	
Kids Cooking	£6.99	
Kids' Cooking Step-by-Step	£6.99	
Low-carb, Low-fat	£6.99	
Low-fat Food for Life	£6.99	
Main Course Salads	£6.99	
Mexican	£6.99	
Middle Eastern Cooking Class	£6.99	
Midweek Meals in Minutes	£6.99	
Mince in Minutes	£6.99	
Mini Bakes	£6.99	
Moroccan & the Foods of North Africa	£6.99	
Muffins, Scones & Breads	£6.99	
New Casseroles	£6.99	
New Curries	£6.99	
New French Food	£6.99	
New Salads	£6.99	
One Pot	£6.99	
Party Food and Drink	£6.99	
Pasta Meals in Minutes	£6.99	
Quick & Simple Cooking	£6.99	
Rice & Risotto	£6.99	
Saucery	£6.99	
Sauces Salsas & Dressings	£6.99	
Sensational Stir-Fries	£6.99	
Simple Healthy Meals	£6.99	
Simple Starters Mains & Puds	£6.99	
Slim	£6.99	
Soup	£6.99	
Stir-fry	£6.99	
Tapas Mezze Antipasto & other bites	£6.99	
Thai Cooking Class	£6.99	
Traditional Italian	£6.99	
Vegetarian Meals in Minutes	£6.99	
Vegie Food	£6.99	
Vegie Stars	£6.99	
Wicked Sweet Indulgences	£6.99	
Wok Meals in Minutes	£6.99	
TOTAL COST	£	

Mr/Mrs/Ms _____

Address_____ Postcode_____

Day time phone _____ email* (optional) _____

I enclose my cheque/money order for £ _____

or please charge £ _____

to my: ☐ Access ☐ Mastercard ☐ Visa ☐ Diners Club

Card number ☐☐☐☐ ☐☐☐☐ ☐☐☐☐ ☐☐☐☐ ☐☐☐☐

Expiry date _____ 3 digit security code *(found on reverse of card)* _____

Cardholder's name_____ Signature _____

To order: Mail or fax – photocopy or complete the order form above, and send your credit card details or cheque payable to: Australian Consolidated Press (UK), ACP Books, 10 Scirocco Close, Moulton Park Office Village, Northampton NN3 6AP. phone (+44) (0)1604 642200 fax (+44) (0)1604 642300 email books@acpuk.com or order online at www.acpuk.com
Non-UK residents: We accept the credit cards listed on the coupon, or cheques, drafts or International Money Orders payable in sterling and drawn on a UK bank. Credit card charges are at the exchange rate current at the time of payment. **Postage and packing UK:** Add £1.00 per order plus £1.75 per book. **Postage and packing overseas:** Add £2.00 per order plus £3.50 per book. All pricing current at time of going to press and subject to change/availability.
* By including your email address, you consent to receipt of any email regarding this magazine, and other emails which inform you of ACP's other publications, products, services and events, and to promote third party goods and services you may be interested in.

TEST KITCHEN
Food director Pamela Clark
Test Kitchen manager Belinda Farlow
Senior home economist Kimberley Coverdale
Home economists Emma Braz, Naomi Scesny, Kelly Cruickshanks, Sarah Hine, Sarah Hobbs, Allison Webb
ACP BOOKS
General manager Christine Whiston
Editorial director Susan Tomnay
Creative director Hieu Chi Nguyen
Designer Michele Withers
Director of sales Brian Cearnes
Marketing manager Bridget Cody
Business analyst Rebecca Varela
Operations manager David Scotto
Production manager Victoria Jefferys
International rights enquiries Laura Bamford
lbamford@acpuk.com

ACP Books are published by ACP Magazines a division of PBL Media Pty Limited
Group publisher, Women's lifestyle Pat Ingram
Director of sales, Women's lifestyle Lynette Phillips
Commercial manager, Women's lifestyle Seymour Cohen
Marketing director, Women's lifestyle Matthew Dominello
Public relations manager, Women's lifestyle Hannah Deveraux
Creative director, Events, Women's lifestyle Luke Bonnano
Research Director, Women's lifestyle Justin Stone
ACP Magazines, Chief Executive officer Scott Lorson
PBL Media, Chief Executive officer Ian Law
Produced by ACP Books, Sydney.
Printed by Dai Nippon Printing in Korea.
Published by ACP Books, a division of ACP Magazines Ltd, 54 Park St, Sydney; GPO Box 4088, Sydney, NSW 2001.
Ph: (02) 9282 8618 Fax: (02) 9267 9438.
acpbooks@acpmagazines.com.au
www.acpbooks.com.au
Australia Distributed by Network Services, phone +61 2 9282 8777 fax +61 2 9264 3278 networkweb@networkservicescompany.com.au
United Kingdom Distributed by Australian Consolidated Press (UK), phone (01604) 642 200 fax (01604) 642 300 books@acpuk.com
New Zealand Distributed by Netlink Distribution Company, phone (9) 366 9966 ask@ndc.co.nz
South Africa Distributed by PSD Promotions, phone (27 11) 392 6065/6/7 fax (27 11) 392 6079/80 orders@psdprom.co.za
Canada Distributed by Publishers Group Canada phone (800) 663 5714 fax (800) 565 3770 service@raincoast.com
A catalogue record for this book is available from the British Library.
ISBN 978-1-86396-556-9
© ACP Magazines Ltd 1999
ABN 18 053 273 546

The publishers would like to thank the following for their assistance:
Fred Bare™
Tupperware®
Tommee Tippee®
Send recipe enquiries to: askpamela@acpmagazines.com.au